BETTER LIVING THROUGH CHRIST

The BOOK OF HEBREWS

LAYMAN'S BIBLE STUDY COURSE

by

JOHN H. SCHAAL

BAKER BOOK HOUSE
Grand Rapids, Michigan

Standard Book Number: 8010-7904-7

Library of Congress Catalog Card Number: 68-57683

The Bible text in this publication is
from the American Standard Version, unless
otherwise designated.
It is recommended that
other translations, including some of the
modern versions such as *Good News for Modern Man,*
The Amplified Bible, or *The Living New Testament,*
also be consulted for more
detailed shades of meaning.

Printed in the United States of America

Preface

Although the study of the Word of God is often neglected, there are signs in these interesting and crucial days of the space age that an increasing number of people are consulting its pages for answers to the problems of society and the individual. More and more Bible clubs and Sunday evening study groups, as well as individuals, are searching in depth for instruction and enlightenment from its inspired teachings.

The book of Hebrews presents Jesus Christ as the superior and only Lord and Savior to an affluent age. The Hebrew Christians were beginning to be sorely tested because they had turned from long-standing Judaism to the despised Christ as their Savior. These impending threats and tests led to the danger of apostasy. The author therefore seeks to prove Christ's claim to superiority, at the same time presenting a strong challenge to the readers to shape up and live courageously for Christ and the faith. Our situation in many ways is similar to the one which faced the Hebrews.

As one studies in some depth and sees Jesus as the better mediator, he will receive inspiration and strength for the future. For the genuine Christian, the tomorrows that lie ahead will demand more and more sacrifice and self-denial, as he lives in this scientific, searching world.

Hebrews also emphasizes covenantal theology — definitively posited in this book and strongly fortified by the Old Testament. This truth is still a basic verity and also a reassuring one for the Christian, since understanding it pledges him comfort and strength. God today has His chosen, covenantal people whom He keeps secure and safe from all powers of apostasy and evil. When trials do come, the Christian — because he is God's covenant child — knows that God is his Father. As his Father, God loves His child, keeps him, and guarantees victory.

It is hoped that a study of the entire Bible, the book of Hebrews, and this study book will enrich the reader's view of that covenant God here portrayed through His Son. This assurance will make the Christian live and witness more gloriously and joyously. Should one who is not a Christian stay "turned on" to read these pages, it is hoped that he will find this God, through Jesus Christ and the Holy Spirit, as his personal Savior and Lord and definitely commit himself to Him.

JOHN H. SCHAAL

Instructions

Instructions for Using This Study Guide

The basis of this study is the Word of God: infallible, relevant, and rewarding when one reads it diligently and prayerfully. The more one depends on its eternal resources, the more help he will receive to face the stupendous challenges and critical times of the space age. The Christian of every age is a witness for Christ (Isa. 43:10; Acts 1:8); and the better he obeys the teaching of the Bible, the better he will be able to live in obedience to the will of the heavenly Father. Witnessing and living to the praise of God is a glorious task, but the more consistently one witnesses, the more certainly he will face testings and temptations similar to those that confronted the Hebrew readers.

The Christian, however, has the assurance that "this is the victory that overcometh the world, even our faith" (I John 5:4b). Of that triumphant faith the book of Hebrews has much to say; therefore, in order to ground the modern-day Christian in that faith and to teach him more of the covenant God's dealings with His children and the wicked world, this study in the book of Hebrews was written. As you begin your study, be sure you stand in a living, born-again relationship with the Christ who is revealed to us in Hebrews as the better mediator through the Holy Spirit.

How to Study

1. The Bible is the main source book; these pages are supplemental tools. Before reading the lesson chapter, read the entire Bible book at least once. Make this book of Hebrews a part of your thinking and living.

2. Consult the Old Testament references and, preferably, the parallel teachings in the Old Testament books.

3. If possible, do some reading on the meaning of the covenant, faith, sacrifices, and law.

4. Read the entire lesson on each chapter of Hebrews; then concentrate on the subjects that need further clarification. After reading the lesson once or twice, look at the questions so that you can refer to them as you read the Bible chapter.

5. Pray and meditate on the material and study when you have a quiet time. By all means ask God's Spirit to guide you. If you are engaged in group study, read the Scripture aloud as individuals or members of the group.

6. Do not become discouraged. The Bible states, "But if any of you lacketh wisdom, let him ask of God, who giveth to all liberally and upbraideth not; and it shall be given him" (James 1:5).

7. It will be helpful to read the Scripture chapters from one of the modern, trustworthy Bible translations. In that way the words will become more meaningful.

8. Make your material relevant by repeating it, thinking on it, and using it in your witness and work for Christ. Discuss the material with others, particularly if this is a group study.

9. Secure a durable Bible if you do not have one, preferably one that has a concordance and some lesson helps. Do not hesitate to mark it with colored pencil or pen.

Materials Useful for Study

(You will be able to do a good job with just your Bible, using the cross-references and concordance, should you not have the materials listed below.)

1. A Bible dictionary and a general dictionary.

2. Commentaries on Hebrews and on the entire Bible for study in greater depth.

3. Bible outline books, background books, maps, pictures, visual aid materials, and colored pencils are good but not essential.

You will receive rich rewards by studying first of all your Bible, then the supplementary explanations, and then writing out the exercises.

If you are enrolled in a correspondence course, ask whatever questions you may have when you send in your answers and share the benefits of your thinking as the Holy Spirit guides and enlightens you.

Personal Record

(Since this book is designed for a person who wishes to study the book of Hebrews either by himself or in a group, this page is for a personal record. The page is also prepared for the student who may be enrolled in one of the classes or may be taking this course through a correspondence division.)

Name ____

Address ____

Telephone number ______________________

City and State _________________________________ Zip code___________

Date course was begun ________________ Date completed ____________

Comments about the course ______________________________________

____

Texts memorized with dates:

a. ________________ e. ________________ i. ________________

b. ________________ f. ________________ j. ________________

c. ________________ g. ________________ k. ________________

d. ________________ h. ________________ l. ________________

(Scripture memorization is important for continued appreciation of the Bible. Make it a point to memorize at least a dozen texts.)

Texts that apply to witnessing or essential points of doctrine are:

a. ________________________ f. ________________________

b. ________________________ g. ________________________

c. ________________________ h. ________________________

d. ________________________ i. ________________________

e. ________________________ j. ________________________

Contents

lesson 1

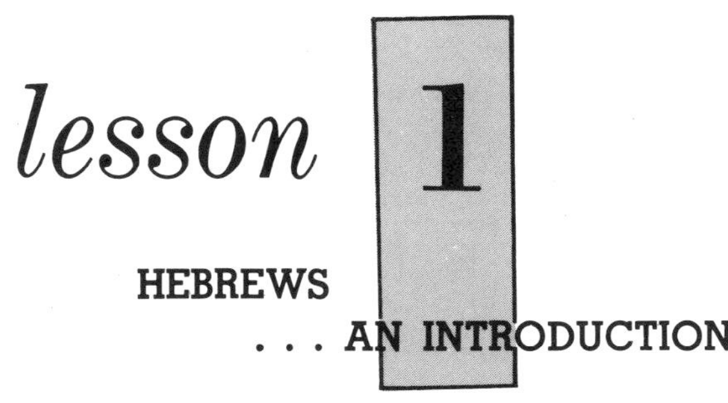

HEBREWS

... AN INTRODUCTION

Who is not interested in better living? The modern world is geared to making life pleasant and good. Actually, there is only one good life and that is found in Jesus Christ. The message of Hebrews is centered around the term "better,"* showing how Jesus Christ is the better Savior offering the better Christian life. The Hebrew Christians had hoped that when they were converted and had vowed their allegiance to Christ their life would be better, but all the persecutions and testings they endured seemed to be a far cry from the promised better life. In these thirteen chapters the writer of the letter to the Hebrews is showing step by step that Christ indeed gives His followers the better life.

As you read the book, answer these questions:

1. Do I honestly have "the better life"?
2. Am I willing to take a stand for Christ and suffer for Him?
3. Am I a joyous, victorious Christian?
4. Do I truly live for the praise and glory of God, constantly crucifying my old life and nature?
5. Am I struggling to let go of the carnal life and am I setting my goal on the eternal life?

A frequent reading of the book of Hebrews will be rewarding and will help you to answer the above questions.

Like the book of Genesis, Hebrews begins in heaven. Christ is seated victoriously at the right hand of God the Father (Heb. 1:3). The readers of that day — so tried and discouraged that they were ready to call it quits as far as defending the faith and staying true to the gospel were concerned — and the readers of today (who are also in grave danger

---

*The term "better" in the book of Hebrews should be viewed in the light of the other concepts with which it is used. It is always linked with one other word or thought. When Jesus is spoken of as better than the angels, better than Moses, better than the Old Testament sacrifices, it is always in comparison with one other concept. When the entire field is covered one needs to speak in terms of "the best." The grammatical comparison is "good, better, best"; and out of this whole discussion in Hebrews, Jesus Christ is the best. To state anything less than that would be to dishonor Christ. In that light too the title of this book, *Better Living through Christ,* is chosen in contrast to non-Christian, legalistic, selfish or even shallow carnal living. The dedicated Christian life is the best of all ways of life since it is grounded in the best mediator, Jesus Christ.

of apostasy) are told right at the beginning that Christ is the victorious Lord. Serving that Christ in spite of opposition and doubt guarantees the readers spiritual victory just because they are in Christ.

Today Christians are too often engaged in a holding action, struggling to keep their faith and worrying about losing what they possess in Christ. Hebrews challenges them to move ahead, to work progressively with joy, knowing that they are indeed "more than conquerors" with Christ.

Purpose of Hebrews

There are at least four reasons why this letter was written. The first was to show the superiority of the revelation in the New Testament over the revelation in the Old Testament by presenting the superiority of Jesus Christ, the Incarnate Word, the great high priest, the mediator of a better covenant, over all the revelations, types, and prototypes of Him found in the Old Testament. Hebrews shows that Christ is the last word, the highest revelation, while Old Testament prophets, priests, kings, sacrifices, offerings, covenants, and laws — though good and glorious in themselves — were but foreshadows and pictures of this coming Christ.

Second, the Epistle was written to strengthen and build the Hebrew Christians in their spiritual life and doctrine in order that they would stand strong in the day of impending persecution and subtle apostasy. Christianity was being tested, as it will be tested again; and some of the Hebrew converts were wondering whether it was really worthwhile to be a Christian. That worthwhileness the writer to the Hebrews demonstrates.

The third reason for writing Hebrews was to deepen and develop the teaching of the covenant. The term "covenant" is used more than a dozen times in this book. Elsewhere it is used most often in Paul's writings. Read such references as Acts 3:25; 7:8; Romans 9:4; 11:27; II Corinthians 3:6, 14; Galatians 3:15, 17; 4:24; Ephesians 2:12; and also Revelation 11:19. There is also a reference in Luke 1:55 in the Song of Mary.

Hebrews deals so much with the covenant because a true covenantal conception is necessary in order to see how God, through Jesus Christ and the Holy Spirit, has woven us into His family, His people, and His church. As His children we shall be equipped in a better way to withstand the terrible testings and temptation to fall away, as well as the hot persecutions and hatreds, because we know that Jesus Christ will sustain His covenant people, giving them grace to resist and stand true.

In the fourth place this book was written to set forth a specific kind of revelation, to a specific group of people who needed this specific teaching — that of warning. This book is replete with hortatory expressions, severe warnings, and definite injunctions earnestly to defend and preserve the faith.

Readers of Hebrews

Some commentators state that the book was written to Gentile readers. Most students believe, however, that those addressed were

Hebrew Christians, since the writer assumed that his readers were thoroughly steeped in a knowledge of the Old Testament teachings and practices. Those who contend that the readers were Gentiles state that these readers had heard the gospel from Jews who had been very close to the Christ when He was upon earth. These Hebrew Christians had instructed the Gentiles in the practices and doctrines of the Old Testament. These Gentiles then had been instructed by the apostles or early ambassadors and associates of Christ. The readers are definitely second-generation Christians, having had no actual, personal contact with Christ in the flesh. That is evident from Hebrews 2:1 which reads, "Therefore we ought to give the more earnest heed to the things that were heard." This is further borne out by Hebrews 2:3: "which having at the first been spoken through the Lord, was confirmed unto us by them that heard."

Much can be learned about these readers by going through the epistle.

1. These readers not only heard the gospel, but that hearing was confirmed by God Himself, "both by signs and wonders, and by manifold powers and by the gifts of the Holy Spirit" (2:4) and by the good tidings preached to them (4:2).
2. They were all "partakers of the heavenly calling" (3:1) and were, in a measure at least, partakers of Christ (3:14).
3. They had a great high priest (4:14; 7:26 ff.; 8:1 ff.).
4. They had the first principles of Christ (6:1).
5. They were those who had done works of love in the Lord's name, and they had ministered to the saints (6:10).
6. They had been enlightened in previous days, enduring persecution and ridicule, yet were compassionate to the less blessed (those in bonds) and joyfully bore the loss of possessions (10:32 ff.).
7. They had not yet resisted to blood (12:4).
8. They belonged to the faithful to the salvation of their souls (10:39).
9. They were provided a better thing by God than all the Old Testament heroes of faith (11:40).
10. They were compassed about by a great cloud of witnesses (12:1).
11. They were come to the heavenly city of God (12:22).
12. There was a danger of their falling away because of persecution (6:12; 10:36; 12:4-16).

From the above, the evidence leans toward the conclusion that the readers were Jewish Christians who had for a while given good witness for their faith, but now needed to be warned because there was a danger of their falling away.

The Author

Actually, no one knows who the author is. Hebrews is most commonly attributed to Paul, but there are arguments both for and against his authorship. Scholars who are against the Pauline authorship state that the form and the style of the letter are not Paul's. The content, too, as to theological ideas and ideas of salvation, is different from Paul's way of reasoning.

Although the authorship is uncertain, these facts are established: The letter is written in excellent Greek and the language shows a scholarly author. The author did not receive the revelation of the contents directly from the lips of Christ; hence he is a second-generation author (Heb. 2:3). The writer appears to be familiar with Paul's teachings, evinced in his knowledge of the covenant, revelation, and other doctrines as portrayed particularly in Galatians.

If Paul did not write Hebrews, who are some of the possible authors? Various scholars ascribe it to Barnabas, Luke, Clement, Apollos, Silas, or Aquila and Priscilla. Whoever the author may be, and we do not know, we are thankful to God for him and for the work he left us through the guidance of the Holy Spirit. As to the style of the book someone has said, "Hebrews begins like an essay, proceeds like a sermon, and ends like a letter."

The location of the recipients of the letter is variously given as Jerusalem, Palestine, and now of late, Rome. If it was the last-named city, there must have been a community of Christian Jews existing in the Eternal City at that time.

Date

As to the time of its writing, estimates from beyond A.D. 50 to as late as A.D. 96 have been given. A date around A.D. 65 would fit, for this was shortly before the destruction of Jerusalem and Nero's persecution (A.D. 64). Also, the severe persecutions suffered by the Christians under Domitian could bring the time of the writing to A.D. 85.

Relation of Hebrews to the Other Epistles

The Just	Shall Live in Him	Victoriously by Faith	With Christ Pre-eminent	In Joy
Romans	Ephesians	Hebrews	Colossians	Philippians

Without the Works of the Law	And Without Trouble and Quarreling
Galatians	Corinthians

In the Blessed Hope of the Lord's Return	In Glory and Majesty
Thessalonians	Revelation

With the above sketch the main content of the various epistles can be visualized.

Fruitful Rewards for Studying

In reading the book of Hebrews and letting it speak to modern-day readers, there are a few main concepts to bear in mind —

The superiority or "betterness" of Christ. The author compared Christ to the Old Testament rituals and worship. Today man-centered, luxurious, materialistic living, together with the rapid advancements of science, all make the Christ of this epistle almost passé. The fact is, however, that underneath our highly advanced and specialized life, there is a sense of emptiness. In the midst of all the remedies and opiates offered, Christ still stands as the only sure anchor of hope.

Understanding that the Word of God is our source of knowledge. This is one of the books that has much to say about "the Word of God" as it is expounded from the Old Testament revelation. The writer does not speak on his own authority but on the authority of God's Word and revelation. With both pulpit and pew neglecting the Word today as the divine source of our thinking and conduct, making man's word authoritative in its place, it is important that we listen to the Word of God and keep it central and normative in our thinking and acting.

Strength in facing suffering and persecution for Christ. As one studies the teaching of Hebrews in terms of the cost of Christian discipleship and the commitment involved, he discovers that suffering, bloodshed, and even death will be increasingly more common for the Christian as the age draws to an end. It was just because the Hebrews were facing opposition, and were concerned about the tests and trials that faced them that they were beginning to backslide and return to their old way of life, no longer willing to pay the price of Christian sacrifice. The writer of the book has some strong statements on this count and exhorts the readers to be true to their confession.

Progressing in the Christian life. The book of Hebrews is written as an encouragement, showing that the Christians have all the gifts of grace, tools of operation, advantages, and assistance needed to move forward in faith. This book is an incentive because Christ is the superior mediator, priest, builder, king, and encouragement to go on to greater heights and conquests of faith.

Emphasizing an eternal existence after death. Our age is not conducive to thinking about life after death. We have it so good that we're satisfied to stay here forever. The fact is that when trials and afflictions hit us, often only then are we inclined to think ahead to what is coming. Neither does the modern emphasis on social betterment and economic affluence make us heavenly minded. The book of Hebrews helps the readers to think more intently on eternal things.

Appreciating the value of the covenant. The aim of the writer is to demonstrate that the New Testament, the new covenant which God made with His children through the promises and sacrifice of Christ, is far superior to the old covenant, the Old Testament. Now God, through the Holy Spirit, has entered into an actual, living, and loving relationship with His people far superior to that of the Old Testament, which pointed forward to this new relationship. This is one of the basic reasons why Christians should live close to God in spite of tests and should progress in sanctification. It is the natural response to this living relationship established by Christ in the New Testament.

Vocabulary and Key Words of the Book

Every writer has his favorite words and expressions. In marking the words that are used repeatedly in Hebrews one can better understand the author's thought.

Better is the first word, and as we trace it through we shall see how the writer points out the superiority of the New Testament revelation, Christ, over the Old Testament revelation.

1. "Having become by *so much better than the angels,* as he hath inherited a more excellent name than they" (1:4).
2. "But, beloved, we are persuaded *better things* of you" (6:9).
3. "But without any dispute the less is blessed of the *better*" (7:7).
4. "(For the law made nothing perfect), and a bringing in thereupon of a *better hope,* through which we draw nigh unto God" (7:19).
5. "By so much also hath Jesus become the surety of a *better covenant*" (7:22). In this connection, Christ is presented as a better priest than the Old Testament priests; and the reasons are also given why He is better.
6. "But now hath he obtained a ministry the more excellent, by so much as he is also the mediator of a *better covenant,* which hath been enacted upon *better promises*" (8:6). The thought here is that Christ's superiority is demonstrated as the head of the covenant of grace, in contrast to the covenant of law and the covenant of nature of the Old Testament. The promises which are better in the New Testament are the fulfillments in Christ of the types and shadows set forth in the Old Testament.
7. "It was necessary, therefore, that the copies of the things in the heavens should be cleansed with these; but the heavenly things themselves with *better sacrifices than these*" (9:23). The sacrifices of the Old Testament had to be repeated constantly, while the sacrifice of Jesus Christ was once for all.
8. "For ye both had compassion on them that were in bonds, and took joyfully the spoiling of your possessions, knowing that ye have for yourselves a *better possession* and an abiding one" (10:34).
9. "But now they desire a *better country,* that is, a heavenly: wherefore God is not ashamed of them to be called their God; for he hath prepared for them a city" (11:16). That, too, is a rather constant thought in Hebrews which is looking forward to the eternal habitation in heaven. Christianity is abiding. It will not pass away, as did the ritual and worship of the Old Testament. Those observances were temporary until Jesus Christ ushered in the permanent and eternal.
10. "Women received their dead by a resurrection: and others were tortured, not accepting their deliverance; that they might obtain a *better resurrection*" (11:35). There were resurrections in the Old Testament, but they were temporary, looking forward to the resurrection in Christ and the resurrection at the end of time when all would be resurrected, never to die again.
11. "God having provided some *better thing* concerning us, that apart from us they should not be made perfect" (11:40). The better thing is the full and complete salvation that we obtain in this better, superior Christ who is our great mediator.

12. "And to Jesus the mediator of a new covenant, and to the blood of sprinkling that speaketh *better* than that of Abel" (12:24). This "better" refers to a better testimony that is more easily understood, for Christ Himself made it plain to us.

Because covenantal teaching is so important in the book, here is the frame of reference in which the term "covenant" is found:

1. "But now hath he obtained a ministry the more excellent, by so much as he is also the mediator of a better *covenant*, which hath been enacted upon better promises" (8:6).
2. "For if that first *covenant* had been faultless, then would no place have been sought for a second" (8:7).
3. "For finding fault with them, he saith, Behold, the days come, saith the Lord, that I will make a new *covenant* with the house of Israel and with the house of Judah" (8:8).
4. "Not according to the *covenant* that I made with their fathers in the day that I took them by the hand to lead them forth out of the land of Egypt; for they continued not in my *covenant*, and I regarded them not, saith the Lord" (8:9).
5. "For this is the *covenant* that I will make with the house of Israel after those days, saith the Lord; I will put my laws into their mind, and on their heart also will I write them: and I will be to them a God, and they shall be to me a people" (8:10).
6. "In that he saith, A new *covenant*, he hath made the first old. But that which is becoming old and waxeth aged is nigh unto vanishing away" (8:13).
7. "Now even the first *covenant* had ordinances of divine service, and its sanctuary, a sanctuary of this world" (9:1).
8. "Having a golden altar of incense, and the ark of the *covenant* overlaid round about with gold, wherein was a golden pot holding the manna, and Aaron's rod that budded, and the tables of the *covenant*" (9:4).
9. "This is the *covenant* that I will make with them after those days, saith the Lord: I will put my laws on their heart, and upon their mind also will I write them" (10:16).
10. "Of how much sorer punishment, think ye, shall he be judged worthy, who hath trodden under foot the Son of God, and hath counted the blood of the *covenant* wherewith he was sanctified an unholy thing, and hath done despite unto the Spirit of grace?" (10:29).
11. "And to Jesus the mediator of a new *covenant*, and to the blood of sprinkling that speaketh better than that of Abel" (12:24).
12. "Now the God of peace, who brought again from the dead the great shepherd of the sheep with the blood of an eternal *covenant*, even our Lord Jesus" (13:20).

The word *partakers* also occurs several times and this word expresses union, oneness. It implies association with and sharers in common experiences — in this case with Christ and fellow Christians. Here is a list of the texts that speak of being partakers:

1. "Since then the children are sharers [partakers, AV] in flesh and blood, he also himself in like manner *partook* of the same; that through death he might bring to naught him that had the power of death, that is, the devil" (2:14).
2. "Wherefore, holy brethren, *partakers* of a heavenly calling, consider the Apostle and High Priest of our confession, even Jesus" (3:1).
3. "For we are become *partakers* of Christ, if we hold fast the beginning of our confidence firm unto the end" (3:14).
4. "For as touching those who were once enlightened and tasted of the heavenly gift, and were made *partakers* of the Holy Spirit" (6:4).
5. "But if ye are without chastening, whereof all have been made *partakers*, then are ye bastards, and not sons" (12:8).
6. "That we may be *partakers* of his holiness" (12:10).

Another word that occurs frequently is *perfection*. We often limit this word to mean being without sin. Perfection means fullness, completeness, spiritual maturity, and is achieved only to the extent that we are completely and fully in Christ. *Heaven* and *eternal* are other words used frequently.

Warning Words. Many warnings are contained in the book —

1. "Therefore we ought to give the more earnest heed to the things that were heard, *lest* haply we drift away from them" (2:1). The injunction is to listen to the voice of God which spoke not only in the Old Testament, but also in the latter days through Jesus Christ Himself.
2. "Take heed, brethren, *lest* haply there shall be in any one of you an evil heart of unbelief, in falling away from the living God" (3:12). Here the danger and fear of apostasy are set forth. That injunction is most appropriate today also.
3. "But exhort one another day by day, so long as it is called Today; *lest* any one of you be hardened by the deceitfulness of sin" (3:13).
4. "Let us fear therefore, *lest* haply, a promise being left of entering into his rest, any one of you should seem to have come short of it" (4:1).
5. "Let us therefore give diligence to enter into that rest, that no man [*lest* any man, AV] fall after the same example of disobedience" (4:11).
6. "Wherefore lift up the hands that hang down, and the palsied knees; and make straight paths for your feet that [*lest*, AV] that which is lame be not turned out of the way; but rather be healed" (12:12, 13).

7. "Looking carefully *lest* there be any man that falleth short of the grace of God" (12:15).
8. "*Lest* any root of bitterness springing up trouble you, and thereby the many be defiled" (12:15).
9. "*Lest* there be any fornicator, or profane person, as Esau, who for one mess of meat sold his own birthright" (12:16).

These warnings ought to teach that "life is real and life is earnest," particularly the Christian life; yet the life in Christ is the better life — in fact, the best.

HEBREWS AT A GLANCE

Chapter 1:1-14

Jesus as God's divine Son is superior to the angels, for He is their creator and master while they are His and man's ministering servants.

Chapter 2:1-18

We should take heed lest we who deserve condemnation neglect the great salvation Jesus gained for us or slip away through temptations and trials.

Chapter 3:1-19

Jesus Christ is superior to Moses because He is the eternally faithful maker and master over His house while Moses was, at best, a temporal faithful servant.

Chapter 4:1-16

There is a rest set aside for those who dwell in Christ. To obtain it, believers need to hold fast their faith in the ascended high priest and come confidently to His throne of grace for help.

Chapter 5:1-14

Christ qualified as high priest because He was God's Son and eternally fit after the line of Melchizedek. He had compassion on men since He too suffered and died. After having done the task perfectly, and having risen from the dead, He became the author of salvation to those who obediently believe in Him.

Chapter 6:1-20

For a partaker of the heavenly gifts to fall away and not live for Christ makes rehabilitation impossible. Because Christ obtained the promised redemption, we have as an anchor of the soul the eventual realization of this redemption.

Chapter 7:1-28
The high priest, Melchizedek, is surpassed by the eternal priest Jesus Christ for He made a once-for-all sacrifice which is eternally sufficient for sin.

Chapter 8:1-13
We possess this eternal high priest who now sits majestically in the heavenly dwelling not made with hands. Because He is triumphant we have living, warm hearts instead of dead, stony hearts.

Chapter 9:1-28
Earthly worship filled with external rituals is done away in Christ and replaced by warm, heavenly worship. The latter is superior because Christ secured the covenant promises of life and peace which we now possess.

Chapter 10:1-39
Jesus Christ, the successful high priest, having once-for-all sacrificed for sin, now sits triumphantly at God's right hand, there sanctifying His saints and preparing them for heaven.

Chapter 11:1-39
The sinner responds to this Christ through faith. The character and conduct of faith is illustrated through its heroes who, tested and tried, remained faithful even unto death.

Chapter 12:1-28
The believing saint is to run with patience the Christian race, looking to Jesus and following the instructions He gives. Heeding God's voice and orders is essential, otherwise one experiences the wrath of God by falling away. But better things are in store for those who hear.

Chapter 13:1-25
God is pleased when His saints remember His rules of conduct and follow them. In their own strength this is impossible; but Jesus Christ, eternally the same, gives them endurance and power. To those who are strong, the benediction of the God of peace rests on them and the great shepherd of the sheep will provide them with every good thing.

HEBREWS
Lesson 1
Questions, Topics, Suggestions for further study

1. The central word of the book of Hebrews is ....
    It refers first of all to the central figure in the book. He is................. .
    Another word that marks Him also is ....

2. What do you think is the purpose of the book?

3. Write out the four reasons why Hebrews was written:

    a.

    b.

    c.

    d.

4. Who were the readers?

5. List five marks of the readers with texts describing them:

    a.

    b.

    c.

    d.

    e.

6. State five rewards for studying the book:

   a.

   b.

   c.

   d.

   e.

7. List and memorize four texts that deal with the word "better."

   a.

   b.

   c.

   d.

8. List other words that occur frequently and indicate where they are found.

9. What, to your thinking, do the references to the covenant want to teach? List several ideas which you have discovered.

   a.

   b.

   c.

   d.

10. Read the book through at least once. Then list some new thoughts you have obtained or some questions you hope will be answered as you continue studying.

   Write as many answers as possible in the blank areas but if you need more space feel free to add a separate sheet.

Is there some central thought that expresses the main ideas of the book and therefore makes it easier to remember the central teaching that better living through Christ is real? Here are several suggestions:

1. Jesus Christ, the covenant leader, guarantees the superior way of life even to those who are weak and subject to persecutions and temptations.
2. Christianity is superior because Jesus Christ is "better" than any person or thing the Old Testament or the world has to offer.
3. Better Christian living is achieved through Jesus Christ, the mediator of the better covenant.
4. The superiority of Christ and the new covenant brings about the better life in Christ.
5. Jesus Christ is the superior high priest and covenant head.

All these suggestions recognize that central to the book of Hebrews is Christ, the superior —

1. Covenant head.
2. High priest.
3. New Testament author.
4. Author and perfecter of our faith.
5. Sovereign sustainer in time of need.

This conclusion can be drawn in summary: Jesus Christ, the covenant Son of God, is superior over all; hence, the way of life, salvation, and the help He presents is superior. Therefore those who are in danger of falling away will find all their strength in Him. Terrible judgment awaits them if they become untrue and fall away.

Because this Christ is superior to the Old Testament prophets, priests, kings, covenants, angels, sacrifices, and laws — because He is "better," He is worthy of our deepest honor, adoration, devotion, and service. To apostatize after having given allegiance to Christ is to fall into evil ways and to experience terrible calamity.

Key Verses

"And to Jesus the mediator of a new covenant, and to the blood of sprinkling that speaketh better than that of Abel" (12:24).

"Having then a great high priest, who hath passed through the heavens, Jesus the Son of God, let us hold fast our confession. . . . Let us therefore draw near with boldness unto the throne of grace, that we may receive mercy, and may find grace to help us in time of need" (4:14, 16).

"Now in the things we are saying the chief point is this: We have such a high priest, who sat down on the right hand of the throne of the Majesty in the heavens" (8:1).

The Three Musts of Salvation in Hebrews

". . . All things are cleansed with blood, and apart from shedding of blood there is no remission" (9:22).

"And without faith it is impossible to be well-pleasing unto him; for he that cometh to God must believe that he is, and that he is a rewarder of them that seek after him" (11:6).

"Follow after peace with all men, and the sanctification without which no man shall see the Lord" (12:14).

The Book's Message

The Hebrew Christians were in danger of falling from the faith into unbelief and worldliness as it manifested itself in materialism and even physical lust and passion. These Hebrews in the New Testament were in the same danger that the Old Testament children of Israel were in the wilderness. They murmured, rebelled, and fell victim to carnality and worldliness, losing sight of the eternal God who had promised refuge and help.

At least two pressures were brought to bear on these Hebrew Christians. The first was that of social influence and prestige, which demanded a conformity to a standard of worldliness to keep in the good graces of that society. The second was the pressure of persecution, which is always a testing for any group. When a group has achieved a measure of respectability and standing, those join it who like that kind of recognition. When the going gets rough, such fall away. The writer is warning against that danger.

This can be seen from such expressions as "drifting away" (Heb. 2:1), "neglect" (2:3), "from an evil heart of unbelief, in falling away from the living God" (3:12), "disobedience" (4:11), and "dullness of hearing" (5:11). The writer was trying to pull his readers from those sins and lead them to "diligence" (6:11), "boldness and patience" (10:35 ff.), and to the "lifting up of the hands that hang down" (12:12).

The "Let Us" Passages

The writer wants to impress his readers with the necessity of remaining true to the faith that gives the better life, so they will not fall away. His method of impression is seen in the frequent use of the phrase "let us." There are at least thirteen of these expressions scattered through the book.

1. "Let us fear" (4:1).
2. "Let us therefore give diligence to enter into that rest" (4:11).
3. "Let us hold fast our confession" (4:14).

4. "Let us therefore draw near with boldness unto the throne of grace" (4:16).
5. "Let us press on unto perfection" (6:1).
6. "Let us draw near with a true heart in fulness of faith" (10:22).
7. "Let us hold fast the confession of our hope that it waver not" (10:23).
8. "Let us consider one another to provoke unto love and good works" (10:24).
9. "Therefore let us also . . . lay aside every weight, and the sin which doth so easily beset us" (12:1).
10. "Let us run with patience the race that is set before us" (12:1).
11. "Let us have grace, whereby we may offer service to God with reverence and awe" (12:28b).
12. "Let us therefore go forth unto him without the camp, bearing his reproach" (13:13).
13. "Let us offer up a sacrifice of praise to God continually" (13:15).

The book of Hebrews stresses the superiority of Christ. Since the readers were supposed to be Christians, they should serve that Christ faithfully and well. But in reality they were not doing this. The writer therefore is concerned about their indifference. He fears that apostasy may come and sternly warns against it. The danger of apostasy is that men may hold intellectually to the true doctrines but in their walk depart from the faith. Apostasy is the opposite of walking by faith. Men are not apostate first of all because of wrong doctrines (that is heresy), but they are apostate even when at first they hold the true doctrine but refuse to live by it. Apostasy is the abandoning of that which one has voluntarily lived by and professed. Of course, if a man does not walk rightly, he will certainly not believe rightly. The two go hand in hand.

Choice Passages from Hebrews
1. The lowly Christ was born as a child to redeem His covenant people, including children (2:10-15).
2. The promise of rest and peace (4:3-11).
3. The glorious high priest (4:14—5:10).
4. The spiritual — New Testament covenant (8:8-13).
5. The spiritual — new sacrifice (9:11-20).
6. The spiritual heroes of faith (chap. 11).
7. The spiritual race (12:1-4).
8. The beautiful spiritual benediction (13:20-21).

BRIEF OUTLINE OF HEBREWS
Introduction: The doxology-praise of Christ's eternal glory (1:1-3).
I. Christ's majestic superiority over God's creation (1:4—2:18).
II. Christ's glorious superiority over Moses and the law (3:1—4:13).
III. Christ's sacrificial superiority over the priesthood (4:14—10:18).
IV. Christ's faithful superiority because He is the author and perfecter of our faith (10:19—13:19).
Conclusion: The benediction (13:20-25).

EXPANDED OUTLINE OF HEBREWS

Introduction: *The glory of Christ, the anointed one, is described* (1:1-3).

   A. He is anointed — prophet ("hath at the end of these days spoken unto us in his Son"). As prophet:
     1. He is heir of all things (1:2b).
     2. He is creator of all things (1:2c).
     3. He is the revealer of all things.

   B. He is anointed — priest ("made purification of sins"). As priest:
     1. He upholds all things (1:3b).
     2. He made purification for our sins (1:3c).

   C. He is anointed — king ("He sat down on the right hand of the Majesty on High").
    As king, He is the ruler (1:3d). Hebrews 1:1-3 contains the introduction of the book and also the main teachings in essence. The ideas set forth in these verses are worked out in the balance of the book.

I. *Christ possesses majestic superiority over God's creation* (1:4–2:18).

   A. He is superior to the prophets.

   B. He is superior to the angels (1:4).
     1. Angels were venerated by the Jews particularly for the part they played in the life of the patriarchs (Abraham, Isaac, and Jacob) and in the giving of the law.
     2. Superiority of Christ over the angels is brought out by seven references to the Old Testament Scriptures. Here, as several commentators point out, is a sevenfold witness to the superiority of Christ over the angels.
       a. Psalm 2:7 and II Samuel 7:14 refer to the Son in His incarnation.
       b. Psalm 97:1-7 refers to Christ's coming.
       c. Psalms 45:6, 7 and 104:4 refer to His exaltation.
       d. Psalm 102:25-27 refers to His rule.
       e. Psalm 110:1 refers to His triumphant judgment at the end of time.

   C. He is superior in His humiliation (2:6-18)
     1. He was humiliated by taking on the form of man and suffering and dying, yet He was eventually crowned with glory and honor (2:9).
     2. He suffered as the captain of our salvation, yet in that way made the sons of glory to be complete (2:10).
     3. He became a child so He could redeem children from bondage (2:14), making salvation real to those of all ages.
     4. He took on Abraham's seed, and was made like His brothers so He could be their merciful and faithful high priest (2:16, 17).

5. He was tempted so He could deliver those that were tempted (2:18).

Conclusion: Though He was deeply humiliated, yet in the background and shining through that humiliation was His glory. This glory was so great that it could not be hidden.

II. *Christ possesses glorious superiority over Moses and the law* (3:1–4:13).

(Christ is superior to Moses as the Son is superior to the servant in the Father's house: 3:3.)

A. He is faithful to God as Moses was faithful to God (3:1-3).

B. The first reason for Christ's superiority is that He Himself is the master-builder of the church (3:6).

C. Christ is superior in teaching and leading out His people for He knows who are His. Moses, being human, did not fully know who were unfaithful among those he led.

D. The readers are warned against unbelief, which was fatal to the followers of Moses (3:7-19).

E. The readers are urged to seek that rest which Joshua and David did not obtain for their people, but which Christ made certain for His people. He thereby assured them that they will attain that heavenly rest (4:1-13).

III. *Christ possesses sacrificial superiority over the Old Testament priesthood* (4:14–10:18).

A. He is superior because He is the great high priest who passed through the heavens (4:14).
   1. He can still be touched by our infirmity (4:15a).
   2. He was tempted like us only without sin (4:15b).
   3. We, sinners that we are, have access to the mercy seat (4:16).

B. As our high priest, He is superior because:
   1. He was called of God, not merely as Aaron, but as God's Son (5:1-5).
   2. He was obedient, thereby becoming the author of eternal salvation, a thing Aaron could not do (5:8, 9).

C. Christ's priesthood is superior to Aaron's because Christ's is patterned after the order of Melchizedek (5:10).
   1. That priesthood after the type of Melchizedek is higher than the Levitical priesthood because tithes were given by the patriarch Abraham (7:5, 6).
   2. Christ is not a priest after the law of fleshly commands, but after the order of eternity (7:3).

3. Christ's priesthood is superior because His priesthood is unchangeable, holy, harmless, undefiled, and made in the highest heavens (7:24, 26).

D. This high priest is described further (8:1-6) as:
1. Reigning at the right hand of God (8:1).
2. Obtaining a more excellent ministry (8:6a).
3. The mediator of a better covenant (8:6b).

E. The priest and the better covenant contrasted (6:6—10:18).
1. The old, faulty covenant is contrasted with the new, faultless one.
   a. The latter is an inner spiritual covenant in the heart.
   b. The former had ordinances of divine services and a worldly sanctuary, with all of its external furnishings.
2. The second tabernacle was not made with hands. It is a holy place in heaven, into which Christ entered after having offered Himself for the sins of His people (9:11-15).
3. The superiority of Christ, the high priest, is demonstrated because He made remission of sins once for all, through the shedding of His blood (10:10).

IV. *Christ possesses superiority because He is the author and perfecter of our faith* (10:19—13:19).
This part is also called the practical part of the book because it consists of exhortations, warnings, examples, and injunctions to faithful Christian living. They are:
A. Boldness to accept these promises of forgiveness and holy living because of the work of the superior Christ, set forth in the first part (10:19-25).

B. Warnings as to what will happen if we depart from the faith (10:26-31).

C. Injunctions to live after the example of the heroes of faith, looking to Jesus for help (11:1—12:2).

D. The necessity of chastisement in the light of persecution and the danger of falling away (12:3-29).

E. Exhortations to duties (13:1-9) in personal and family life, in doctrine, in religious life, and in prayer.

Conclusion: The benediction (13:20-25).

HEBREWS

Lesson 2

Questions, Topics, Suggestions for further study

1. Give one theme of the book of Hebrews that you have memorized. Could you suggest a theme of your own?

2. Write from memory either a key verse or the three "must" verses.

3. Who is Christ?

   a.   d.

   b.   e.

   c.

4. List some expressions that convey the dangers confronting the readers.

   a.   d.

   b.   e.

   c.   f.

5. Write a paragraph on the exhortations. What conclusions are there to the "let us" admonitions?

6. How do you define apostasy?

7. What is your choice passage from Hebrews? (This assumes you have read the entire book as preparation for this lesson.) Indicate why you have chosen that passage as your favorite one.

8. What is a doxology?

9. Who is a "hero of faith" and how can he be described?

10. Discuss the concept of superiority as applied to Christ and give examples.

11. Try to give in your own words a brief outline of Hebrews.

GOD SPOKE ... THROUGH CHRIST

Hebrews 1

I. God has revealed Himself through Christ, who is "better" than all creation (vss. 1-3).

II. This Christ is also "better" than the angels (vss. 4-7; 13, 14).

III. This Christ's throne is eternal amid a changing heavens (vss. 8-12).

Note the quotations from the Old Testament in this chapter:

Verse 4 — Psalm 2:7   Verse 10 — Psalm 102:25-27
Verse 5 — II Samuel 7:14   Verse 13 — Psalm 110:1
Verse 7 — Psalm 104:4

Chapter 1 opens by assuming God's Being and reality as a Person, just as Genesis does. The basic assumption is that he who reads will have to "believe that God is" and that He is a Person. Only then will he see aright what God has in store for him.

At three strategic spots in the Bible, the individual books open with the concept of God. There is a progressive revelation in the presentation. In the first book, Genesis, we read, "In the beginning God created the heavens and the earth." That first chapter records God speaking in eternity within the Trinity. God spoke and the world came into being — a pure and holy world. Man, however, broke his communion and fellowship with God; but God continued speaking in the Old Testament through various channels as the book of Hebrews here points out.

The New Testament opens with God again speaking, for John 1 tells us that the Word became flesh and that that living Word spoke. However, men again rejected Him and nailed Him to the cross. The Epistles, written during the post-resurrection period, show God speaking still.

The book of Hebrews, as a third progressive impact, has God again speaking. In chapter 1:1, 2 we read, "God, having of old time spoken unto the fathers in the prophets by divers portions and in divers manners, hath at the end of these days spoken unto us in his Son." Now God speaks through His Son from heaven and through His Holy Spirit who proceeds (and speaks) from the Father and the Son and dwells in us.

The problem in the book of Hebrews was that the readers were becoming alarmed at the trials that appeared in the offing and therefore were in danger of slipping away from the faith. They should heed God's voice calling them back, because it is better to hear His voice calling in love and for commitment and obedience than to hear Him speak in judgment. God's voice will definitely be heard by everyone, either in love or in judgment.

The judgment aspect of God's speaking comes up later in the book. If men do not heed the pleading, loving voice of God, the results will be tragic. Hebrews 12:25 states, "See that ye refuse not him that speaketh. For if they escaped not when they refused him that warned them on earth, much more shall not we escape who turn away from him that warneth from heaven."

The chapter continues with the statement that "God of old times spoke" to the fathers and in the latter times spoke through Christ. How did God speak in the old times? He spoke "in the prophets by divers portions and divers manners," that is, by —

1. Prophets and through the schools of the prophets.
2. The sacred writings of those prophets, preachers, and men of God.
3. The offerings and sacrifices which were lessons spoken to them through God.
4. Signs and wonders and miracles of diverse kinds and character.
5. Urim and Thummim.
6. Dreams and visions.
7. Angels and theophanies.
8. The law.
9. The conscience.
10. His general revelation.

The emphasis of the chapter is that God spoke. He interrupted the silence of the previous four centuries and spoke once again, pouring out His message to men. This speaking was unique for it was a speaking through His Son; it was a speaking in and from human flesh through the incarnation. The added message is that Christ spoke "when he had made purification of sin." He spoke also by actions. In fact, in a sense God had spoken in all the ages; but in the New Testament times He spoke through His Son. Since our age is still the "last days" He is still speaking through His Son. Today He does so through the Word as it is explained and applied to our hearts through the Holy Spirit and through His church in action.

That Christ is living today and that the Word of God is living is declared by Peter in I Peter 1:23, 25: "Being born again, not of corruptible seed, but of incorruptible, by the word of God, which liveth and abideth forever. . . . But the word of the Lord endureth forever. And this is the word which by the gospel is preached unto you."

One of the purposes of the book in proving the superiority of the Christ comes out in its opening verses. Notice these points from verses 2-4:

1. That Christ "is the heir of all things" certainly shows His great possessions together with the Father (vs. 2).
2. Christ is the creator of the world: "by whom also he made the worlds" (vs. 2).
3. Christ is "very God of very God . . . of like substance with the

Father" (Nicene Creed); "who being the effulgence of his glory, and the express image of his substance" (vs. 3).

4. Christ is the providential sustainer of the universe He made (vs. 3), "upholding all things by the word of his power."
5. Christ is the purifier of our sins (vs. 3).
6. Christ is the exalted ruler (vs. 3).
7. He is better than the angels (vs. 4).
8. He has a more excellent name than they (vs. 4).

We see in these verses that Christ is all in all: prophet (vs. 2), priest (vs. 3), and king (vs. 3). Implied in these verses is His deity, His incarnation, His atonement, and His ascension.

Chapter 1 also shows that Christ is superior to the angels because of the fact that God the Father called Christ "his Son." He never addressed the angels that way. Because God is truth and cannot lie, to address someone as His only begotten Son makes Him superior to the angels. By way of parenthesis, since we too are called the sons of God through our having been begotten in Christ, we too are superior to the angels. Our superiority is not due to ourselves but to what Christ did for us.

The Scripture here is establishing Christ's Sonship and deity, consequently showing His superiority over the angels. This the Father wanted clearly established, for twice God spoke from heaven in an audible voice calling Christ His Son. The first took place when John baptized Jesus at the Jordan. The voice from heaven declared, "This is my beloved Son" (Luke 3:22). The other occasion was the transfiguration. Then added emphasis was given to the revelation, for the Father not only said, "This is my beloved Son," but added, "Hear ye him" (Luke 9:35). God wanted to establish firmly that —

1. Christ is one with the Father. John teaches that in John 17:22: "And the glory which thou hast given me I have given unto them; that they may be one, even as we are one." Such oneness does not exist between God the Father and the angels. This oneness became quite a struggle in early religious history and is known as the Arian controversy. The conclusion of that struggle brought out the Nicene Creed about the year A.D. 352. This creed declares that Christ is "very God of very God; begotten, not made, being of one substance with the Father."

The Jews had a strong conviction in the role of angels, believing they could do many things for them. Christ was the despised Jew, the hated Nazarene. Some wondered whether, in time of persecution and affliction, angels might not be more effective for them than Christ, who had Himself been persecuted and put to death. Because of that worry the writer is showing the superiority of Christ over the angels.

2. Christ is co-creator and co-laborer with the Father in creating and redeeming the world. The angels, of course, are not. There is sufficient evidence in Scripture to prove this assertion, particularly John 1:1 ff.
3. The Word was made flesh so that we have, according to the Scriptures, Immanuel, God with us, for our salvation, proving that

God is here on earth revealing Himself to men. True, angels were also on earth, but they did not and could not do what God did. He obtained our salvation for us, and the angels were His ministers. Angels, after all, revealed God and are our ministering servants. Jesus Christ was God and revealed Himself.

In the light of the above — for the salvation which Christ obtained was also for the angels — the angels worship Christ. Christ is, therefore, superior on the count of worship, too, for we may worship no one save God alone and Christ is God. That is the injunction of the Old Testament, particularly the moral law which the Jews tried to follow with great solemnity. "The Lord God shalt thou worship and him only shalt thou serve" applies to all of God's creation, including the angels. Since Christ is admittedly (by the Father's own word) God, we worship Him. Angels may not be worshiped nor may they worship themselves.

In the balance of the chapter, another comparison is drawn between the angels and the Son. The Son is the everlasting King, He is the most highly exalted One. The angels in comparison are at the opposite end of the pole: they are ministering servants. In a sense the comparison goes from one extreme to another. Christ is supreme, is King; the angels are even lower than man. How then can we become so twisted that we exalt the creature higher than the Creator? Romans refers to the sin men commit who think themselves greater than God and worship the creature rather than the Creator.

As ministering servants, the angels rejoice because they are filling the purpose for which God created them. Beyond that calling they can never go; nor do they want to, because they are absolutely obedient to do the will of God. What do the angels do?

1. The angels are busily engaged working for God, for this very Christ who some seemed to think was inferior to them. They serve God by:

    a. Proclaiming messages of good tidings, as in the case of Gabriel and the angelic host that announced the birth of Christ (Luke 2) and the angel at the empty tomb (Matt. 28:2).

    b. Conveying messages and carrying out commands of judgment, as the angel who brought death on the host of the Assyrians (II Kings 19).

2. They are permitted by God to be used as our servants, too. They are used in our protection, and according to several writers there are guardian angels. That view is based on Matthew 18:10: "See that ye despise not one of these little ones; for I say unto you, that in heaven their angels do always behold the face of my Father who is in heaven."

Certainly God uses the angels, who serve Him, to be ministering servants in our behalf. They are engaged in serving us as Christ's ministers, particularly in the sphere of protection from material and spiritual evils, and also helping in the realm of mercy. Most likely they do not serve in the realm of grace. They definitely are not ministers of the gospel, a task that is reserved for man.

Much of the proof of the superiority of Christ over the angels is taken from the Old Testament, which is quoted by the writer to the Hebrews. There is logic in that type of presentation. These readers were great believers in the Old Testament. What better procedure could the writer follow than to prove his points by quoting directly from the sacred writings? In that way the reader would not be overthrowing the writer's arguments if he disbelieved, but would be casting aside the very Word of God. A pious Jew would not quickly do such a thing.

The chapter closes by telling us we are heirs of salvation. As used in the Scriptures, the word *salvation* has three meanings:

1. Believers have been saved, that is, have been taken from a life of sin and made the recipients of marvelous grace. They are no longer hellbound, but are traveling heavenward. In that sense salvation is a definite, specific act which God has accomplished. Believers are redeemed from the guilt and judgment of sin.

2. Salvation is continual, constant, over-and-over deliverance from sin. Believers are daily being delivered from evil. In that sense salvation is on-going until death. The process of sanctification enters at this juncture. Believers are also in the process of being saved.

3. Complete salvation is received in full only when the kingdom of Christ is ushered in at the end of time. With such victory assured, there can be no better life than that.

❊   ❊   ❊   ❊

TEXTS, NOTES, and IDEAS

TEXTS, NOTES, and IDEAS

HEBREWS

Lesson 3

Questions, Topics, Suggestions for further study

1. Why does this writer use so many Old Testament quotations?

2. Restate the main thought of Hebrews.

3. Enumerate some of the ways by which God spoke.

   a.   e.

   b.   f.

   c.   g.

   d.   h.

4. Although this is not in the notes, state what it means that "God spoke."

5. Give some thoughts on Christ's superiority.

   a.   d.

   b.   e.

   c.   f.

6. What is the main work of the angels?

7. Why may we not pray to or worship angels?

8. Write briefly on the "angels as ministering servants," giving at least two thoughts on the subject.

9. What does the term "salvation" mean?

10. What does it mean that we are "heirs of salvation"?

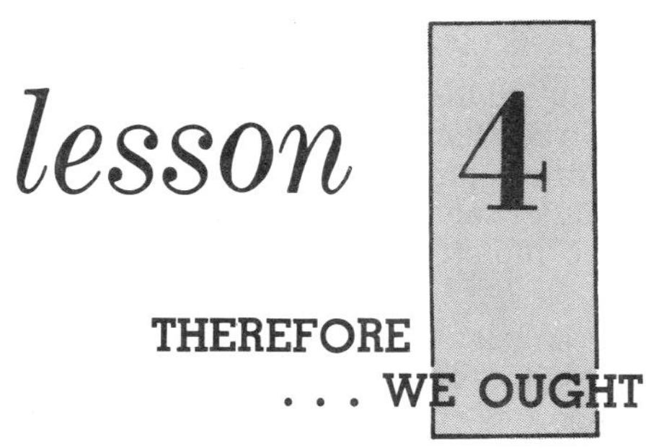

Hebrews 2

I. Take heed, lest we drift and be lost (vss. 1-3).

II. God's witness of man's superiority over the angels (vss. 4-8).

III. God's exaltation of His glorious Son (vss. 9-18).

    A. He was humiliated to bring sons to glory (vss. 9-12).

    B. He was born a child to redeem fearful flesh (vss. 13-15).

    C. He became like men to qualify as a merciful high priest (vss. 16, 17).

    D. He was tempted in order to help the tempted ones (vs. 18).

Chapter 2 begins with an exhortation that takes up the first four verses. That exhortation is the result of the preceding portrayal of Christ's superiority over the Old Testament and the angels, as is seen from the "therefore" with which the chapter opens. Why "ought we to give the more earnest heed to the things we have heard"? The answer is that the revelation which is given in the Son is so much more outstanding than that given in the Old Testament, and because the Son is so much more worthy than the angels.

Further, this revelation of the New Testament was not brought by the angels, as was the case in the Old Testament, but was brought by the One who is superior to the angels, God's Son, Jesus Christ. Because He is so worthy, we ought to give heed to the worthy revelation that comes from Him. In the fact of God becoming flesh, we have a majestic revelation and an overwhelming grace. It is a terrible thing to drift away from that truth, not to be absorbed by that fact, and not to lay hold on it. The clause translated "lest haply we drift away" actually means "lest we be carried away." The danger was that the readers would be washed away from their solid foundation by the strong tide of doubt, temptation, and persecution which was pulling them away from the glorious gospel. Against that the writer to the Hebrews warns.

Another reason for the "therefore" is an implied one. This Son is

God's exclusive hope for our salvation. If we reject Him, there is no other way of obtaining salvation or "the rest" prepared for those who commit their allegiance to Him. As Paul states it, the Christ is the last Adam, and if He had not remained true, there would have been no hope of redemption. With Him we either stand or fall. To think that angels can be of any help in the securing of salvation is not only to settle for the lesser but is to miss salvation completely, because Christ is the one and only source of salvation.

In using the term "better than the angels" one does not yet see the full implication of Christ's exclusive worth. He is the "best" and only One who can redeem. This is the uniqueness of Christianity over against all other religions. Its claims are complete, definitive, and must be accepted totally or one cannot share in the Christian heritage and inheritance.

The purpose of God sending His Son, other than to bring glory and honor to His name, is to restore man through regeneration, salvation, and grace to a relationship of peace and sonship with God. Such restoration can be achieved only by God sending His Son. If that is cast aside or allowed to slip past us, the result is stark tragedy.

The meaning of the word "neglect" is not merely passive, but it means an active departing from those things previously known and confessed. Those things have been part of life and are realities which were formerly treasured and considered as essential for the true Christian life. But now, because of testing, the readers were minded to let them go. In order to keep the readers following Christ and to avoid their falling away, the writer is trying to impress them with the fact that if the word "spoken through angels" was steadfast how much more sure and abiding will Christ's words stand. What words were spoken through the angels? Most commentators say this refers to the law. Even in the giving of the law the angels were the ministering servants. This is evident from such texts as Deuteronomy 33:2, Psalm 68:17, Acts 7:53, and Galatians 3:19.

Notice how much greater is this Word, this revelation that has come to us, than the words spoken through angels:

1. It was uttered by the Lord Himself while He was dwelling on earth.

2. It was proved true by those who heard that word. The saints who believed in Jesus' day and showed by their life the power of that word are exhibits of its truth.

3. God Himself proved its truth by backing it up with miracles.

4. Another proof was demonstrated by the gifts and fruit of the Holy Spirit as set forth in I Corinthians 12-14 and Galatians 5:22, 23. The gifts of the Spirit are visible demonstrations that this word is powerful. Those Hebrews were in danger of flouting all, in spite of the mighty array of evidence. In the light of all that, for any person to say that he isn't impressed or he doesn't think the facts warrant Christ's great claim as the only Savior is folly. Apostasy is a sin that throws evidence to the wind and results from indifference and apathy in spite of the overwhelming evidence offered.

It is the attitude of one who just does not care to see and live by the evidence.

Christ Is Superior and Triumphant in Spite of Humiliation

In dealing with the preceding, Christ was seen as the divine One, superior on several counts. Then came an exhortation to be observed in our atittude toward Him and these divine things. Now we are ready to look at Christ as the perfect man, who took our flesh and was humiliated in order that He could become the captain of our salvation. Man was created by God to control and be the head of the universe, but through sin he became a slave. Christ entered that position of slavery in order that He could take man from that evil and restore him to freedom, bearing nobly the full image of God. To do that He had to suffer. This text states: "for it became him, for whom are all things, and through whom are all things, in bringing many sons unto glory, to make the author of their salvation perfect through suffering" (vs. 10). This eternal, sovereign Son was made lower, for a time, than the angels, over whom He is superior, in order that He could make us perfect.

While Jesus was on earth He was lower than the angels, but even then the angels ministered to Him. All along Christ was destined, after His human life, to be made great and mighty. This was predicted of Him already in the book of Psalms and particularly in Psalm 8, quoted here in the book of Hebrews. In that Psalm His glory was foretold, and this full glory will be completely revealed in the kingdom of glory. As you read that Psalm, it might not appear as if Christ is referred to, but certainly Christ who is the Son of Man was appointed heir of all things by the Father. All is in subjection to Him.

As you study this part of God's Word, ask whether this talk is not too ethereal to be meaningful for down to earth, everyday living. Does it really appear as if the thought of this Psalm is true? When Jesus went to heaven, in fulfillment of the words of this Psalm, He said, "All authority hath been given unto me in heaven and on earth" (Matt. 28:18). Is that really true? Indeed, and this passage in Hebrews gives added grounds to prove its reality: "We see not yet all things put under him." Men are still permitted to rebel against God, to despise His grace, to ridicule His Word and to ignore His Spirit. Men today are called to suffer for righteousness' sake because of the delay in the fulfillment of that promise. But look at conditions and circumstances with the eye of faith: "we see Jesus, now crowned with glory and honor." God, who is longsuffering, is truly exercising all power and authority. For that reason then Christ tasted death and rose again. He did triumph and so do we.

We read in verse 9, "That by the grace of God he should taste of death for every man." The original does not have the word "man." The writer is speaking in verse 8 as follows, "for in that he subjected all things unto him, left nothing that is not subject to him." The writer is speaking about all things. The part under discussion may be translated: "he should taste of death for everything."

Through His death Christ redeemed the cosmos, the universe.

Through His death sinners alone are not only saved, but the whole creation itself is saved now and is to be delivered from the bondage of corruption eventually. Everything in heaven and on earth is to be brought into harmony with God, so that the whole creation will harmoniously praise Him forever. That is the teaching here and that is the teaching of the entire Bible. Christ died to save sinners, but there is more: He died to bring the whole universe into harmony so that the whole universe will glorify Him, "for of him, and through him, and unto him are all things, to whom be the glory forever" (Rom. 11:36). And the larger purpose in saving sinners and redeeming the world was to make the whole universe obedient to the will of God. God in Christ reconciled the world to Himself that the world would serve and praise Him.

For the sake of clarity, let us sum up the material presented in chapter 2 to this point.

1. Redeemed men are to rule the world under the kingship of Christ.
   a. Even though man has been made on some counts a little lower than the angels, this position is temporary, as Christ's humiliation was temporary. Christ's humiliation and final exaltation is the ground of our hope. In essence, through creation and Christ, man is higher than the angels.
   b. Through Christ we have been crowned with glory and honor.
   c. We have been placed over the works of God with all things in subjection because Christ has gained the victory. But as far as we are concerned, as yet this is not actually realized. Our victory is still future. It is certain because it is in the divine plan. To that end we are working and struggling.

2. Christ tasted death in order that He could redeem the world and make this honor of being a King possible and certain for man, that man thereby would properly glorify God.

Christ Is Superior Even Though and Because He Died for Our Sins

The next section of this chapter comprises verses 10-18. It is an explanation of God's purpose in making Christ taste death, which means that He entered into the full, bitter experience of what death really is.

1. It was fitting in order to bring many sons to glory. It answered God's purpose very well to make the captain or leader complete, truly fit, by having Him suffer. It was the God-ordained way to rescue us from the grave through grace to glory. The word "leader" is used four times in the New Testament: here, and in Hebrews 12:2, Acts 3:15, and 5:31. The meaning of the term "perfect," or "make complete," does not refer to His divine nature, but to His being truly prepared for His task as Savior. He becomes identified as our elder brother and He is not ashamed to call us brothers.

2. It was necessary that Christ taste death in order that He could deliver all His children from the fear of death and bondage. Notice how exclusive that removal of fear is: "not to angels," says

the Bible, "but to the seed of Abraham." The seed of Abraham is the spiritual people of God (Gal. 3).

3. In order to obtain our redemption it was necessary for Christ to become like us, in human flesh, in order that He could become our great high priest. He was obliged to take our sinful nature on Himself. At this point we see Christ as the high priest for the first time in the epistle.

   a. The heart of the epistle also has the idea that Christ is the great high priest. This high priest removes all the difficulties our sin has caused between us and God.

   b. This He did through His human suffering, temptation, and death.

   c. Through this God-appointed way, He is able to help, redeem us who are tempted. Christ's loving help goes out to tested and tempted children.

   d. He "is able" to help us and deliver us from the temptation. In studying the various "He is able" passages we see a rich Christ emerging as an asset to the weary Christian, so that with Him life is better.

Chapter 2 closes with its emphasis on the fact that Jesus Christ as the Son of Man is superior to the angels. It has shown us His superiority over the angels as the Son of God.

To Be Forsaken of God.

So great is the hideousness of sin, that God ruled the only way it could be eradicated, was for His Son to pay the full and entire penalty. That penalty included:

1. Shedding His blood as payment to God as the price He demanded for sin.

2. Utter and full rejection as seen in God forsaking His Son. No one had ever gone that way before, but Christ in the garden and on the cross stepped out into complete desolation and came back. This is one of the mysteries of the redemptive plan. How could God be forsaken of God? And He wasn't; yet He was. How could Jesus the man, like us in all things, be forsaken of God and survive — yet He did. What a price God paid for our salvation.

3. A voluntarily assumed obedience on the part of Jesus Christ even to death when He was innocent and should have stayed in heaven but left heaven and became like us in order that He might redeem us.

The Christian Lives Two Lives

The duality in the Christian life has been a worry and concern to the dedicated saint. It shouldn't be, for actually the Christian does appear to lead two lives.

First of all as a born-again person, he is deeply conscious and aware of the greatness of sin. On the other hand he doesn't think about that sin for he clings to the assurance of the Bible which tells him, "your sins and iniquities I will remember no more" therefore, if God does not remember them, why should he be concerned.

That, of course, is easily said, for even though God has removed our iniquities, we are the ones who are the transgressors and have to deal with them constantly. The fact remains, however, that the more we live for Christ, and the more we are aware of what Christ, the mediator, has done, the more we will think about the positive, constructive life in Christ and therefore have less and less time to think of sin.

✷　✷　✷　✷

TEXTS, NOTES, and IDEAS

Lesson 4

Questions, Topics, Suggestions for further study

1. Chapter 2 portrays Christ's superiority over .... and

   the ....

2. What does the term "drifting" mean?

3. Write a brief paragraph on "Christ is better than . . . ."

4. Why should the readers not "neglect so great a salvation"?

5. List reasons why this revelation is great.

   a.

   b.

   c.

   d.

6. Give reasons why the better mediator was humiliated.

7. Explain for whom and why Christ "tasted death."

8. Describe how Christ and we are triumphant.

9. How did Christ bring many sons to glory?

10. Enlarge on the idea of "He is able." Take a concordance and list
    some references that speak of Christ's being able.

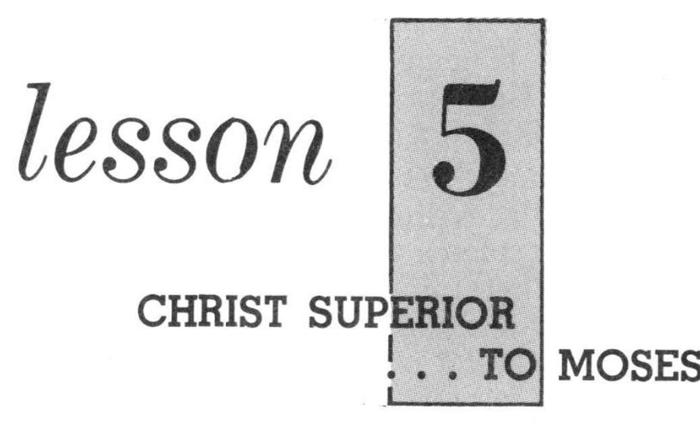

lesson 5

CHRIST SUPERIOR ... TO MOSES

Hebrews 3

I. Christ, the high priest, more glorious than Moses (vss. 1-2).

    A. Because He built the house (vss. 3, 4).

    B. Because He was the Son (vss. 5, 6).

II. Warning to hold fast and not fall away (vss. 5-19).

We have seen that Christ is superior to the angels both on the count of His being the Son of God (chap. 1) and on the count of His being the Son of Man (chap. 2).

Angels are heavenly beings — exalted, aloof, dwelling constantly in glory. The Son of Man is human. He came down from heaven to dwell among us but in this connection He is of the earth, earthy. Chapter 3 brings contact between heaven and earth in offering two thoughts: (1) house, and (2) high priest.

Jesus Christ dwelt here on earth, as did Moses, who on some counts was the first Old Testament type of a go-between, a mediator, and consequently a priest. Moses dwelt in an earthly, movable tent called a tabernacle, or house; and Jesus Christ dwelt in an earthly house. Notice the comparison between these two. Neither one had a permanent, well-built, earthly mansion. Both were wanderers in the land. But the figure in Hebrews is that both were building houses — dwellings not first of all for themselves but for God. Moses built a house — God's people, Old Testament Israel, and Jesus Christ built a house — God's people, called the church in the New Testament.

To convey a further symbolism, those houses needed to keep contact with the head of those houses — God. For that contact a middle man, a mediator, was necessary. For that reason the concept of high priest is also introduced in this chapter.

In chapter 3 the writer shows that Jesus Christ is superior to Moses. Why must Christ and Moses be compared? Moses was held in exceedingly high esteem by the Jewish readers; he was the personification of the law. At the time the law was given, Moses was almost transfigured; and when he came down from the mountain he still reflected the glory of the Lord. As Erdman says in his commentary on Hebrews, "Moses was . . . the very embodiment and glory of the divine revelation and of the old dispensation with which Christ is being compared" (p. 43). This added to his grandeur in the minds of God's people.

One of the points of comparison between Christ and Moses is on the count of faithfulness. For that faithfulness Moses was highly esteemed. He did that which God wished. Says this writer, Jesus Christ was faithful too. Here are two faithful persons, Moses and Christ, both of them faithful to God. Moses, however, was faithful as a servant to his master who was the great builder; Christ was faithful in Himself, for He Himself was the builder of the house. The master is greater than the servant. Such a servant Moses was and such a master Christ was. The contrast is that of a servant and the Lord creator and builder. Of course the Son is the superior one. One expects and can demand faithfulness of a servant. A master is faithful of his own free will. His faithfulness therefore is greater. Such voluntary faithfulness the master Christ gave.

The term "house" is used several times. Moses was faithful over the house as a servant, but God is the builder of all things. Over that house Christ was the master and head. There is the further statement, "Whose house are we."

There are three uses of the term "house":
1. The house over which Moses was faithful was the tabernacle.
2. The builder of the house (of all) is God; this is the entire creation.
3. "Whose house are we" refers to the church of the Lord Jesus Christ, so Christ is King of the universe and Lord of the church. Christ was faithful over the last two, which also indicates His superiority over Moses.

Until one does some comparing, the reason for introducing the thought of a house might seem strange. It will clear up when the question is asked, "What is a house for?" At least two answers can be given. A house is a dwelling, but above all it is a place to which one comes for rest after the struggles with the outside world. The author must have had this thought in mind for he introduces the "rest" concept in the next chapter. Christ gives comfort and rest as well as a dwelling place when one enters the house of which He is the head. On that count He is superior to Moses, whose house was never permanent and stable but was in a constant flux. The Israelites were always on the move, looking forward to their dwelling in the promised land where they were to be given rest.

But Christ should be considered superior not only on the count of faithfulness, but because of His greater dignity and honor. Moses was faithful, but his task was only a small one in comparison to the task and position of the Lord Jesus Christ. He as God had the great task of being King of the world and head of the church. That is seen in these words, "For he hath been counted worthy of more glory than Moses, by so much as he that built the house hath more honor than the house."

A new section begins with verse 7. From chapter 3:7—4:13 there is a series of warnings against unbelief and falling short of attaining the heavenly goal. In chapter 2:1-4 a warning was issued to beware of the peril of drifting, of neglecting so great a salvation. Here the peril of unbelief is present. Since the writer has been discussing Moses he thinks of the people of Moses' day who, because they disbelieved, fell short of reaching the promised land. That example he holds before his readers as a solemn warning.

The method of proof the writer uses is that of showing his arguments to be inspired. He takes his words and arguments directly from the sacred writings, the Old Testament Scriptures. Here the reference is from Psalm 95:7-11. In fact, the writer states that it is the Holy Spirit who speaks these words of warning; hence they are weighty and important. Moses was faithful in the work to which God called him, therefore he must also have faithfully witnessed and warned his people. But his people did not take his warnings or believe his teachings, and so they perished. Christ too was faithful in His task. He warned and witnessed. If one does not hearken to His voice, he perishes eternally. That is the import of these verses. It will be our own "evil heart of unbelief" that condemns us if we will not listen to Him.

From chapters 3:12—4:13 the writer adds his application to the words quoted from the Psalm. The main thrust is "harden not your hearts." One commentator brings out the solemnity of this truth when he states that so earnest is the writer that he shows emphatically how this terrible danger is to be met "in the seven appeals that are made: 'consider' (3:1); 'hear His voice' (vs. 7); 'harden not your hearts' (vs. 8); 'take heed' (vs. 12); 'exhort' (vs. 13); 'hold fast' (vs. 14); 'fear' (4:1)" (W. H. Griffith Thomas, *Let Us Go On*, p. 47).

Chapter 3:12 shows clearly the danger of apostasy, one of the main problems of the Hebrews. This should lead to exhorting and warning one another continually. There needs to be a constant supervision and exercising of discipline over the flock. The *today* is not a reference to a period of time in contrast to yesterday or tomorrow, but rather to the simultaneous time as the voice is being heard. Just because the voice of God speaks now, right now, the reader must hear, heed, and be careful not to fall away. The term *today* gives relevance to the study of Hebrews as it speaks of conditions, dangers, and problems that are the same in our time as they were in the writer's day.

What was the cause of this unbelief in the children of Israel? From the history of their wanderings in the desert, at least three things stand out as the cause of their apostasy:

1. The first one was their murmuring. This was due in essence to a lack of physical things and hence a lack of security. They preferred the security of Egypt more than the insecure life in the wilderness, even though they had the promises and presence of God.

2. The second sin was their disobedience. This was climaxed in Moses' smiting the rock, rather than speaking to it. Moses lacked faith in God's promise for that given moment. He was not trusting God — today. As a result he was disobedient. He took his eyes off God and launched out on his own, showing more trust in his

own ability to get things done. No wonder God dealt so severely with His servant.

Moses was committing the very sin he had been fighting in his people. In fact, isn't that at the heart of unbelief? God makes statements and promises, but we disbelieve them and by our conduct show ourselves disobedient.

> 3. Hand in hand with murmuring and disobedience went "departing from the living God." Circumcision was neglected and the Passover was not celebrated in the wilderness because these people were wandering further and further away from Him who was the source of their life.

This unbelief had a tragic ending for the children of Israel — as it would have for the Hebrews if they were not careful. The carcasses of the covenant people lined the desert roads. Everyone of that generation perished except Joshua and Caleb. A second tragedy was the fact that they did not enter into the land of promise, the land of rest. They were weary, restless souls all their days and at the end perished miserably instead of seeing the calm and rest of the land of Canaan. Unbelief has dire results.

Since this is a spiritual problem, those who disbelieve today will be restless all their days and in the end not enter rest, but eternal restlessness and punishment. Had these covenant people only believed, they would have been able to conquer the obstacles and giants of the new land. Instead they held back and murmured and consequently failed. They did not trust God, and as a result destruction — the very thing they feared *with* God — came to pass because now they were *without* God. The readers of Hebrews are urged to move forward in faith although they were fearful of persecution and experienced obstacles and difficulties, persecutions and scorn. Like the spiritual giants of old, with steadfast faith in Christ as their Head, they would triumph. To fall back into unbelief, however, would mean the realization of their fears.

The writer ends chapter 3 by stating that the evidence was before them that the Israelites could not enter the land of promise because of unbelief. That Exhibit A should be a signal warning to the readers.

Lesson 5

Questions, Topics, Suggestions for further study

1. In chapter 3 Christ is portrayed as superior to ....

2. On these counts Hebrews speaks about .... and ....

3. What meanings can be taken from the term "house" as seen in this chapter?

4. In this chapter Christ can also be called "superior" on these counts:

   a.

   b.

   c.

5. What warnings are spoken of in verses 7-13?

6. What does the Holy Spirit do in this connection?

7. How does one "not harden his heart"?

8. How does one fight against the danger of apostasy?

9. Write on the significance of the term "today."

10. What happened when the people of Israel fell away from God during their wilderness journey?

11. The tragic result of Israel's apostasy was:

lesson 6

THE BELIEVER'S TASK
. . . OBTAIN REST

Hebrews 4

I. The danger of losing the promised rest (vss. 1-13).

II. The Christian's twofold task (vss. 14-16).

Chapter 4 opens with a warning ("let us fear") and a promise (rest) centering around the possibility of the readers' falling short of obtaining rest. Whose or what rest this is will have to be determined by the text and by a look at Psalm 95, which is quoted as part of this chapter. The Scripture reads "his rest" and the reference is to God's rest. We are dealing with God's "heavenly rest," contrasted with "earthly rest." The latter refers to a situation that confronted the children of Israel when they entered the land of promise, which was also known as a land of rest.

On entering the land of Canaan the battles of the children of Israel would be over, their worries and fears abolished, and they could enjoy the fruits of their journeying and conquest. They could "sit down" and live the life of contemplation and praise in thankfulness to God, building a new world with God as their King. The promise God had given them in their state of need and slavery was now achieved. In this chapter we have the first reference to a promise. Jesus Christ is superior because, having given a promise, He will remain faithful in granting it. The danger comes from the readers: will they fulfil the conditions this promise demanded for obtaining the blessings?

The discussion runs like this: We ought to fear and be careful and thoughtful of these things presented in the gospel, lest a promise being left of obtaining a rest, we should still miss it. Now why should they miss it? Because hearing about it alone does not guarantee obtaining it. As the ancient Israelites traveled through the desert, they had the good tidings (gospel) preached to them of entering into the land of Canaan, the land of rest. They heard that message but didn't enter into the promised land, the land of rest, because they only heard and did not actually believe. This showed that they did not live by faith. As a result, they were lost both temporally, that is, they did not obtain the earthly rest, and eternally, that is, they did not enter the heavenly rest. Merely hearing the Word did not benefit them; in fact, it testified against them.

The Israelites apparently believed at the first, for they left the land of Egypt by faith. But they lost what appeared to be a true faith (which actually it was not), and because they lost it in the wilderness, they perished. Says this writer, "You too have come to belief," but beware lest, appearing to have faith, you are like the Israelites: you reach a point and then disbelieve, with the result that the promise will never be obtained because of your unbelief. In Psalm 95 God swore an oath to those unbelievers, that they would not enter into rest. This proves that He intended (from a human viewpoint) that they should enter in, but they did not because God's wrath was kindled against them because of their unbelief.

Those who truly believe do enter into that rest at death. That rest is God's rest which He gives in His love. It was produced by Him and He now shares it so that through His grace His weary children shall obtain it. For God that rest began when He had finished His creation. He rested then and desired that man, His creation, should share in it. Therefore, He gave the Sabbath Day as a day of rest and as a symbol of the eternal rest to come. Because God is in heaven, the rest is definitely the heavenly rest. The victorious pilgrim, the Christian, at death will be ushered into the heavenly rest, which God entered when He had completed the work of creating the universe. Jesus Christ entered that rest when, after His suffering, death, and resurrection He ascended triumphantly into heaven.

The writer to the Hebrews is warning his readers to strive to enter that heavenly rest by believing and working acceptably during their life's journey. The danger was that some of them were apostatizing and were becoming disloyal to the Christ whom they at one time had confessed. For that reason, the writer quotes the example of the Israelites and uses Psalm 95 to show how angry God was in those days. Since He is an unchanging God, He would be filled with wrath if these readers of that day fell into unbelief.

That rest is obtainable today on the same condition as it was in those days — on condition of faith, through grace and forgiveness of sins.

What is that rest? It certainly is not inactivity, but rather a period of peace and calm that comes after labor and struggle. It is a time of blessed communion and fellowship with God, a time of cessation from struggle, a time of appreciation of one another's presence in calm and peace. It is not the rest of inactivity, but rather of finished work.

Just because Israel was excluded from this rest, a place still remains open for us to enter it. In other words, because of Israel's unbelief, the heavenly places have vacancies that we may claim. Here was an incentive to these fearful, slipping readers to take up the struggle with new courage.

The conclusion to this presentation is found in verse 9: "There remaineth therefore a sabbath rest for the people of God." It is for us to enter it. From verses 10-13 the exhortation is given in the confident expectation that we shall surely enter that rest, since it deals with the strength and might of God's Word, that Word written in Psalm 95 and coming to us by divine inspiration also in this letter to the Hebrews.

This Word is quick and powerful and sharper than any two-edged sword, a discerner of the thoughts and intents of the heart. As it used to be stated, the Word is efficacious; therefore the writer is confident that his readers will heed it and as a result enter rest.

One has the right conception of the Word of God when he sees it as living and active. This passage, together with the exposition in I Peter 1:23-25, portrays the Word as alive. It is not simply the print, not the book on a shelf, not even the language spoken or written that make up the Word. Such a word is dead. It is living because it is Holy Spirit breathed. The book, the speech, the words are meaningful when they come alive through the Holy Spirit and become dynamic in the sense of the Spirit working in our lives. Until that happens the Word is a deposit, a treasure, inactive and unused. This living Word is "active" and "sharper than any two-edged sword" just because it is working in the lives of those who speak it, read it, and in the lives of those to whom it comes through the speech, page, and witness of others. This Word penetrates life to the core and discerns the feelings and intents of the heart. When the readers realize the power of that living Word, it will act as a weapon to fight off temptation and trouble. Instead, the readers were lagging and giving up. The writer therefore uses strong encouragement, warnings, and exhortations to tone up the spiritual resistance of his readers.

The second part of chapter 4 introduces the subject of the majestic high priest, Jesus Christ. This new section begins with chapter 4:14, and goes on to chapter 10:18. The overall theme for all these chapters and verses deals with Christ, our mediator, as the great high priest. In this section we are to see the priesthood of Jesus Christ as the Son of God, a priesthood after the order of Melchizedek, and not after the order of the Levitical priesthood, that is, after Aaron's.

In verse 14 the subject of the priesthood is introduced and explained. It was seen before in chapter 2:7 and again in chapter 3:1, but now it is enlarged. Yet it is not fully taken up until chapters 7-9. We have these concepts concerning the high priest: He is faithful and at this point He is presented as merciful. Up to this point we have seen the various aspects of the superiority of Christ. Now the writer will present another aspect of that superiority, that is, a superiority of Christ over the Aaronic priesthood.

This passage tells us three things: We have a high priest — Jesus Christ; He is a great high priest; He has passed into the heavens.

We have a high priest. That means that He was commissioned and was able to offer sacrifices. He alone could do that. In the Old Testament there was one high priest and he alone could offer *the* sacrifice for the people. He offered this sacrifice as an atonement for sin. In our day we cannot offer sacrifices. Someone else has to do that for us. Jesus Christ did. In a sense if He were only a high priest, He would be no different from those who followed in Aaron's train. But the Scriptures go on to say that He is the great high priest, than whom there was no greater and before whom all were inferior.

This high priest is now gone into and through heaven for us to the throne of God. Now we have an advocate, an intercessor, in heaven for us.

Because Jesus Christ is that kind of high priest, He can be touched by our infirmities. Though He was tempted in all things as we are tempted, He did not yield to sin as we so often do. Therefore, even though He is now in heaven, He is strong and able to help us on earth who are weak.

Here is another incentive for the Hebrews to stay true to their Christian confession and life. There is a sympathetic high priest who is triumphantly seated at God's right hand in heaven. He will intercede and present their needs to the Father. It is for them to see these truths and live by them.

In verses 14-16 the writer is presenting the main aspects of theology under a twofold injunction: "Let us hold fast" and "let us come boldly to the throne."

What are we told to hold fast? Our confession, which confesses (a) Jesus to be the human mediator, (b) the Son of God who is divine, as well as (c) the great high priest who sacrificed Himself for our sins. This high priest penetrated the heavens, having ascended, and now is with God. The humanity and deity, as well as the blood theology, are in these verses, as are the facts of the resurrection, ascension, and session on the part of Jesus Christ at God's right hand. To hold fast this confession would evoke temptations, trials, and persecutions; but God would help, hence the second "let us." This confession is the orthodoxy coming out of their hearts and minds and translated into audible testimony.

The second exhortation deals with the practical application of the Christian life. One almost wonders why the readers should be told to come "boldly to the throne." There are at least two reasons:

1. Prayer isn't easy and we might neglect to pray; therefore the writer encourages his readers to pray with power and confidence. But one does not come to the throne of God lightly or easily. In fact, the throne represents judgment. In that light the book of Esther has something to say about the majesty of the king and the fear of the queen in approaching the throne. There is an analogous situation for the Christian.

2. Here the throne is not one of judgment however, but a throne of "grace." Just because it is the throne of grace we are exhorted to come boldly, that is, with confidence and full assurance. At a time of fear we are to approach that throne with assurance. This section ought to encourage the Hebrew readers and us to come with courage and promptness because this is God's throne of grace.

The reason for coming is to obtain mercy, that is, help for the bad situation in which these readers found themselves. It is indeed right to come to God in all of life's situations — the daily needs and troubles included. That is not the only reason for coming, though, but "that we may find grace to help us."

When we come to find grace we have either lost it — and some of these Hebrew readers were in danger of doing that — or we are seeking some higher good. The latter certainly was true for these readers. They needed grace to help them move to higher strength.

The chapter ends with mercy and grace available. It is up to us to seek and find them. We need to seek in the right place and here it is spelled out as the throne of grace. All this, of course, needs to be seen in the light of a correct theology, a theology that is far superior to the Old Testament in that Jesus Christ, the Son of God, the great high priest, is all that we need and exactly what God has promised.

✵ ✵ ✵ ✵

TEXTS, NOTES, and IDEAS

TEXTS, NOTES, and IDEAS

HEBREWS
Lesson 6
Questions, Topics, Suggestions for further study

1. Why did the Israelites fail to enter the land of promise?

2. Define "God's rest."

3. How is Psalm 95 used in this chapter?

4. What incentives are offered in this chapter to the readers so that they will not fall away from the Christian life?

5. Write a paragraph on rest over against inactivity.

6. How should the Sabbath be spent?

7. How did Jesus Christ qualify as a high priest? Why was He superior?

8. What is the Word?

9. Write a paragraph on the theology of verses 14-16.

10. Is it necessary to "exhort" one another today?

11. How does the book of Esther relate here? Read that book and indicate points of help you have received as they pertain to understanding the difference between a "throne of judgment" and a
"throne of grace."

12. Is it easy for a Christian to pray? Give reasons for your answer.
Why the exhortation to come boldly?

lesson 7

JESUS CHRIST
. . . THE QUALIFIED HIGH PRIEST

Hebrews 5

I. Qualified by God's appointment (vs. 1).

II. Works in behalf of man (vss. 2-3).

III. Followed the Melchizedek line (vss. 4-6).

IV. Suffered in the days of His flesh (vss. 7-10).

V. Teaches us in spite of our weaknesses (vss. 11-14).

This chapter explains the thought expressed in chapter 3:17, that Jesus Christ is the sympathetic high priest. If Jesus is the Son of God and greater than any earthly high priest, how can He still associate with and be sympathetic to sinful mortals? The answer is that He has gone through the same course, experienced the same temptations as we, except that He did not yield to them but remained without sin. As a human Savior living among us He was like us and therefore did qualify as our sympathetic high priest.

This chapter deals specifically with two things:
1. The high priest is highly qualified to be the great high priest because He was tempted as we are. The emphasis, however, deals with the qualifications of the high priest in general, rather than specifically dealing with those of Christ (vss. 1-10).
2. The readers' condition is diagnosed as one of spiritual infancy and immaturity, with the result that they cannot take the deeper truths of the Scriptures (vss. 11-13).

In the first part of the chapter the writer confirms the preceding assertion: Christ is our merciful high priest, and therefore we should approach Him with boldnesss. *For* is the connecting word. The writer then states the qualifications of a high priest and shows that Christ has them. Among others, these two qualities are essential to being a high priest: identity with men (vss. 1-3) and authority from God (vs. 4). These attributes Christ possesses as seen in verses 5-8; therefore He is both high priest and Savior (vss. 9-10).

The author discusses the second attribute first: a high priest is appointed by God. He quotes the following Scriptures to prove this appointment: Psalm 2:7, which he has used before (1:5), and Psalm 110:4, which shows that Christ is that high priest. Verse 1 states that the high priest was to offer both gifts and sacrifices for sins.

The Lord Jesus Christ offered the sacrifice for our sins on the cross; but now, in heaven, He is offering the gifts that we bring Him as our thank offerings for His gift of salvation. Further, He is offering for us His completed sacrifice as His gift to God the Father. Our prayers, our offerings are part of the gifts He brings to God.

In verse 2 the author returns to the thought of a merciful high priest, this time in terms of compassion. The reason that Christ can and does have compassion on us is that He "was compassed with infirmity." Further, He was a human priest like Aaron. For that reason, too, He did not glorify Himself, but rather humbled Himself, leaving the giving of glory to His Father. As God's Son He learned obedience by suffering in obtaining salvation for His people.

In the days of His flesh Christ suffered greatly as shown in this passage: "Who in the days of his flesh, having offered up prayers and supplications with strong crying and tears unto him that was able to save him from death, thus learning obedience." All this qualifies Christ, who was "compassed with our infirmity," to be our merciful high priest. In that light the author wants these weak and even backsliding Hebrew readers to be strong and intelligent. He repeatedly urges — in fact, almost goads — them on to better Christian thinking and living (see vss. 11-14).

This chapter teaches that Christ is not first of all a priest of the lineage of Aaron, but one after the order of Melchizedek. Verse 11 opens with the words "Of whom we have many things to say." Commentators differ as to who is meant in that statement. Some want to make it refer to Melchizedek, and then tie it up with the thought that the Jews would not take charitably to the things said about Melchizedek. The reason for this would be because in their legalistic thinking and living they were following the Old Testament pattern of the Aaronic and Levitical priesthood. The sentence appears to refer to Christ, who is being spoken about in this whole paragraph. After all, the writer is only introducing Melchizedek incidentally. It would seem more logical to believe that many things about Jesus Christ were hard to say and were not understood by the readers who were thinking of giving up Jesus Christ, since they by that token showed their weakness and immaturity.

These verses are again an insert or interlude, for ordinarily the writer would have proceeded to deal with the nature of the priesthood of Christ after the order of Melchizedek. Because that is a difficult subject, particularly to babes, he chided them and then encouraged them to better things. The many things the author has to say about this Christ are found in chapters 7—10:18.

These things deal with the fact that he is now speaking of Christ, the actuality, over against the Old Testament, which speaks in terms of types and shadows. He is writing of the full revelation of Jesus Christ over against an incomplete and unfulfilled revelation in the Old Testament. Only those who are mature and strong will be able to understand the new things. Since these readers were practically claiming the superiority of the Old to the New, he thinks they have retrogressed and backslidden. Consequently the new thoughts would be hard to express and difficult to understand.

When Moses was making his farewell speech recorded in Deuteronomy, he stated that God would set a king over His people. He then went on to describe the characteristics that such a king must possess, one of which was that the king was to be "one from among thy brethren" (Deut. 17:15). Here the same mark is applied to a high priest. In the case of Jesus Christ, *the* high priest, He was to be human and like us, His brothers. Several other marks are added: He is to serve or act in behalf of man and He is to offer both gifts and sacrifices. He must bear gently with the ignorant and erring.

In the previous chapter the reader was exhorted to come boldly to the throne, but no man can go as he is in himself. He must come with some credential, some gift. Consequently, here it is shown that Jesus Christ is our high priest who offers for us gifts and sacrifices. Man comes then to the throne of grace through the Person and gifts of Jesus Christ.

The readers of the book should have known all this and should have been teaching this to the novices and new converts. Instead, the writer states that they had not progressed and therefore they themselves needed to be taught again the ABC's of Christian doctrine. Instead of being strong because they had exercised themselves in the deep truths of the Word, they were becoming anemic and couldn't stand the meat of the Word. They needed milk instead of meat. The writer feared they were no more than babes — as proved by their complaining of the difficulty of practicing the Christian religion — and now there was the real danger of backsliding. Hence in the next chapter he challenges them to leave behind the ABC's and to move forward with the work of strengthening and advancing their Christian faith.

※　※　※　※

NOTES, COMMENTS, and OBSERVATIONS

Lesson 7

Questions, Topics, Suggestions for further study

1. List the two things that chapter 5 unfolds.

    a.

    b.

2. Explain the truth that Christ, *the* high priest, offers both gifts and sacrifices.

3. Why can and does Christ have compassion on us and our infirmities?

4. How does this writer bring out the intensity of Christ's suffering?

5. To whom does the statement "Of whom we have many things to say" refer? Give reasons for the stand you take. A good suggestion would be to consult other writers to see what they have to say on this point.

6. Why does the writer need to add verses 11-14? If he had not done so, what subject would he immediately have taken up?

7. What is the meaning of being a "babe"?

8. Give and comment on the several marks of the high priest.

9. Comment on why you think both the king (Deut. 17:15) and the high priest had to be from among the people.

10. Why should these readers have been teachers instead of babes?

11. List some of the truths you have learned as to:

    a. the purpose of the book of Hebrews in your reading up to this point.

    b. the superiority of Christ.

    c. the need of Christ being the high priest that He is.

lesson 8

SPIRITUAL BABES
. . . OR MATURE CHRISTIANS

Hebrews 6

I. Move on beyond the basic spiritual ABC's (vss. 1-3).

II. Take heed not to crucify Jesus Christ afresh (vss. 4-8).

III. Better things are true of Christians (vss. 9-12).

IV. Anchor the soul in hope, obtained through Jesus the forerunner (vss. 13-20).

The situation at the opening of this chapter seems to indicate that the writer is addressing himself to a group of people who had left Judaism and had made some commitment to Christianity. Although they had confessed Christ, they were doubting whether they had made the right choice. In view of the cost involved — testing, temptations, possible persecution and bloodshed — they were glancing at their old religion rather longingly.

The writer is both chiding and prodding them for making no advance either in Christian life or doctrine. They still adhered to the ABC's of the Christian faith, but those fundamentals had also been taught in Judaism. Consequently the writer is saying, "You can't keep on nursing the first principles of Christ. You need to progress and press on to the higher things. You cannot constantly talk about repentance from dead works, faith toward God, baptism, laying on of hands, resurrection from the dead, and eternal judgment."

What's wrong with holding on to these teachings? They are good but they are also basically Judaism's teachings. These are invalid now because they are not Christ-centered. One does not stay with the ABC's beyond the primary grade, but uses those essentials in the process of spiritual education and growth. At that point, chapter 6 opens as the writer prods the readers on to progress.

The problem was that these readers were in danger of reverting to the rudimentary and antiquated teaching of the Old Testament. In spite of Christ's coming and having fulfilled the Old Testament, they were making the Old Testament teachings normative and superior to Christ.

To them, life according to Moses and the law was preferable to the gospel of Jesus Christ. The reason was that they had not fully grasped the superiority of Jesus Christ. The author therefore recalls the basic teachings of Judaism, which indeed form the ground floor and basis of Christianity. But since Christ had come, He shows how the Christian must move on to higher levels. Those who had come out of Judaism had a wonderful heritage, and this is set forth in six items that laid the Old Testament foundation for Christ's coming:

1. Repentance from dead works (vs. 1).
2. Faith toward God (vs. 1).
3. The teaching (doctrine) of baptisms (vs. 2).
4. The laying on of hands (vs. 2).
5. The resurrection of the dead (vs. 2).
6. The eternal judgment (vs. 2).

In the Old Testament God's people were constantly urged to repent from dead works and live in newness of life before God. Ezekiel spoke of God giving His people a heart of flesh as against a heart of stone. The climax of the Old Testament was found in John the Baptist, whose twofold work was that of preaching repentance — that is, doing away with dead works — and washing or baptism unto remission of sins. The people needed to be cleansed and then turn in faith to God. The Old Testament also taught the laying on of hands in the sense of sacrifices for sins and atonement for sin, particularly in the scapegoat that was sent into the wilderness with the sins of the people. Even though some denied the doctrine of the resurrection (Sadducees), it was there in the Old Testament. For example, Psalm 16:10 says: "For thou wilt not leave my soul to Sheol; neither wilt thou suffer thy holy one to see corruption." The judgment, too, is taught in the Old Testament: "For God will bring every work into judgment, with every hidden thing, whether it be good, or whether it be evil" (Eccles. 12:14). Again, we read in Daniel 12:2, "And many of them that sleep in the dust of the earth shall awake, some to everlasting life, and some to shame and everlasting contempt." The Old Testament certainly assumes some division, some judgment going along with a resurrection.

The Christian believer not merely repented from dead works, but was born again through Jesus Christ and definitely believed in God as Savior and Lord. Above all he believed that Jesus Christ is the Son of God, the Messiah, who cleansed him by His precious blood. The Christian, washed through the blood of Christ, the high priest, no longer needed baptisms. He had received one baptism through the Holy Spirit unto the washing away of sin, visibly demonstrated by his water baptism. No longer could there be a laying on of hands, for Christ had paid the price of redemption. As to resurrections, "we have been raised with him to newness of life" (Eph. 2:6), and now we live in the hope of the blessed resurrection when Christ shall come to judge the living and the dead. That is the Christian program, and he who entered the Christian way could never really retrogress. If he did, it was proof that he had never been part of the Spirit-produced life.

That is the difference between the Jewish and the Christian worshiper. Some of these Jewish so-called Christians had outwardly and nominally participated in these things, for they had confessed Jesus to be their anointed Messiah. But because the program of blessings had not arrived as soon as they expected, and because Jesus Christ had not returned to set up His kingdom, and because their faith was external rather than a Spirit-born, heaven-given faith, they were ready to throw overboard the Christian life and return to Judaism. Apparently some had already done that and were now permanently out of the Christian life (see vs. 9; II Thess. 2:3). In that light we can understand the terrible pictures presented in verses 4-8. These people were the apostates, the renegades. True, they appeared genuine; but actually they had never been regenerated, even though they had all the external marks and appeared to have experienced the good gifts of the Holy Spirit.

Verse 4, among other descriptive phrases of these apparent degenerates, states that they "were made partakers of the Holy Spirit." Looking more closely at the references dealing with the Holy Spirit in Hebrews will give a better understanding of this passage.

Texts dealing with the Holy Spirit:
1. "God also bearing witness with them, both by signs and wonders, and by manifold powers, and by gifts of the Holy Spirit, according to his own will" (2:4).
2. "Wherefore, even as the Holy Spirit saith" (3:7).
3. "And were made partakers of the Holy Spirit" (6:4).
4. "The Holy Spirit this signifying" (9:8).
5. "And hath done despite unto the Spirit of grace" (10:29).

The implication of the above passages is that just because these apparent backsliders were a part of the corporate group, included in the visible body of the church or the saints, they too had witness borne to them by signs and wonders. They saw the many powers of the Spirit and were even the external recipients of the gifts of the Holy Spirit just as the rest. The Holy Spirit had spoken to them also and they had seemed to listen. They had obtained the corporate blessings, appropriated them, tasted them, found them good at the time but actually never did fully assimilate and take to heart the genuine gifts. Consequently when troubles came they, not having genuine faith, wanted no part of Christianity. Because they had received so much and were in such close fellowship with the Spirit, if they were now to discard the truth, such action would make it impossible to renew them. They would have gone too far first in the pursuit of the spiritual and then in the discarding of the eternal.

The Apostates Described
1. They had been enlightened in the essentials of the Christian gospel and life. They knew about Jesus Christ's humble birth, His suffering and death, His resurrection, and the way to obtain salvation. They had been enlightened, but the light was not actually in them. For them Jesus Christ was not the Light. They had seen the way, for the light had shone on them and around them — but not *in* them.
2. They had tasted of the heavenly gift but had not actually partaken of the Living Bread. They were so near, yet so far from Christ.

They had chewed and experienced the good taste but had not swallowed and assimilated Christ. He had not become a living part of them.

3. They had been partakers of (recipients of, companions with) the Holy Spirit in an external way. The original text does not have the definite article "the" before "Holy Spirit," so it conceivably may not even be the Holy Spirit who is spoken of here. The meaning then is that they were partakers of a consecrated, a set-apart spirit together with other believers. Or, if the Holy Spirit is the meaning, then the Spirit was theirs only in a general way, like that of Ananias and Sapphira. It was He who had enlightened them through the preaching and unfolding of the Word in the external call, but not actually inwardly and definitely to the point of causing them to yield fully to Him.

4. They had tasted of the good Word of God. Like the parable of the sower, they had gladly accepted this good news when they heard it; but eventually when persecution came, like the seed that had fallen on shallow ground or among thorns, their faith soon withered and choked to death.

5. They had seen the powers of the age to come in the mighty deeds of Christ and the power and the strength of the gospel in human lives; but in spite of all that, they had fallen away.

The picture here is parallel to that of the children of Israel in the wilderness. The Hebrew readers reacted to Christ in the same way the children of Israel had reacted to God in the wilderness — they rejected Him. In rejecting Christ, they were rejecting the superior One, the One who alone would be able to help and give them peace and security. They chose rather the outmoded, outdated religion of Judaism, which was not able to save them.

The crucial fact is that these apostates had "crucified to themselves the Son of God afresh." That does not mean an actual crucifixion, by which Jesus Christ could historically be hung on a tree again and shed His blood a second time, for Christ had been raised from the dead and ascended into heaven. No man or nation could physically lay hands on Him, for He shed His blood, died, rose again, and was now in heaven beyond their reach physically. Rather, these individuals had experienced, in a sense, the good of Christ's death; but now, as they turned back to Judaism (which really hated Christianity), they individually were spitefully re-enacting an event in history. They were crucifying Jesus in their souls. Such sin has a horrible end: "whose end is to be burned." The expression "to be burned" is found only here in the New Testament in connection with the judgment. It is one of the most somber and terrible pictures ever presented of the doom of the individual apostate. Burning is the sure end of all men who crucify anew Jesus Christ for themselves.

It may well be that the writer is setting forth this passage as a hypothetical case and not as an actuality. He wishes to be realistic and stern in his warning and, therefore, paints the blackest picture possible. He is virtually saying that if it were possible for those who were once enlightened to fall away, it would be impossible to renew them unless Christ would go through the whole process of dying a second time. That, of course, would put Him to an open shame; for it would negate all His previous work and all that had been promised and posited of Him.

Another commentator writes: "The (above) interpretation is plausible as is seen in the use of the third person such as, 'those,' 'they,' and 'them,' while in verse 9 the writer returns to the personal address and appeal, showing that the writer thinks better things of his readers." Since the writer is addressing babes in Christ, he may be speaking plainly and drastically to warn them and to show them in plain language the impossible situation that confronts them if they do not progress. They will either be guilty of the sin he describes or they will move forward. He knows the latter will be true if they are really Christians. Further, the definitive word "impossible" can only refer here to a definite, strong-willed, hard-hearted apostasy. This falling away then is a long hardening process. The writer trusted this would not be true of his readers.

After the serious passage on apostasy had been written, the writer saw the need of adding warning and exhortation. The best remedy for apostasy, says he, is to live close to Christ and to keep busy in Him. This is the remedy for so many things. If a man begins to doubt, let him get busy in the things of the Lord and his doubt takes wings. If a man is endangered by apostasy, let him work hard in the things of the kingdom.

To be occupied and busy with Christ means at least five things. (1) It means learning to know His mind and His will from the Word. Then, knowing it, (2) the Christian will have to get busy putting it into practice. To do that (3) he will need help from God through His Spirit, and that help (4) he will seek through prayer. Added to all this is (5) the exercise of meditating on the things of Christ. If a person does not do that he is in mortal peril and, as Erdman says, "No peril can compare with that of falling away from Christ and despising the gospel of His grace and love" (*Commentary on Hebrews*, p. 66). But, as the writer says, "we are persuaded better things of you." There were some good marks about these readers. They had done some fine work and God would not forget that. Now the writer is exhorting them to continue in that way of life and not to go back to Judaism, regardless of the cost to them. He desired to see them continue steadfast to the end.

We have now reached the second part of the chapter. What has preceded presented a severe and solemn picture, but not a hopeless one. The hope is seen in God making a promise to Abraham, whose seed (spiritually as well as physically) these readers were; and God would live up to the promise He had made. From this the readers could take strong encouragement since they hoped in that faithful covenant God. The writer wishes to be most emphatic on that point, too, so he says that God confirmed this covenant to Abraham with an oath. W. H. Griffith Thomas has this observation, "It is interesting to notice the three divine oaths in this Epistle: one referring to non-believers (3:11); one to Christians (6:13); and one to Christ (7:21)" (*Let Us Go On*, p. 78).

Hope is described in verse 19 as an anchor of the soul, the only such reference in Scripture. This anchor had been carried within the veil by Jesus Christ in His completed work of atonement. As a result, hope is steadfast and sure. Writers are quite agreed that Jesus acts as our forerunner, which thought contains a maritime concept of a small boat in a Mediterranean harbor. In the harbor there was a huge, immovable rock near the shore. That rock served as an anchor for boats, but at low tides ships could not get to it because of the shallow water. Then the anchor of the large ship would be placed in a small boat, called the forerunner, and carried over to the rock to which it would be tied. Tying the anchor of the ship to the rock would make it "fast and sure." Jesus Christ certainly did that very thing, for no one would be able to be anchored in the safety of the harbor by himself. We are safely secured within the harbor, tied securely by Christ Himself.

Chapter 6 closes by showing Jesus, the "forerunner," entering the harbor, heaven. He is described as a secure and strong forerunner. Melchizedek, who appears first in Genesis, is used as a symbol of Christ's greatness, as he was one who had no beginning or end. That is, he appeared to be eternal since the emphasis in his case is not on origin or parenthood (as was the case with Aaron) but on his priestly, sacrificial work. Jesus Christ, it is stated, became a high priest forever after Melchizedek's order. The writer, who has referred once before to this priest, in chapter 5:10, is now ready to enlarge on that thought. He does this in chapter 7, showing there that Christ is even superior to the priesthood of Melchizedek.

❊ ❊ ❊ ❊

PRAYER REMINDERS

HEBREWS
Lesson 8
Questions, Topics, Suggestions for further study

1. What current problem faced the readers of this epistle?

2. Contribute your thoughts on evidence that a person is:
   a. an immature Christian

   b. a mature Christian

3. State various levels of Christianity, basing your answers on Scriptural proof. See, as an example, I Corinthians 3.

   a.   c.

   b.   d.

4. Which six items did these readers believe? Why was that not enough?

   a.   d.

   b.   e.

   c.   f.

5. What are the elements of repentance? Show what is the meaning of the thought that we need repentance. Is repentance necessary for salvation in this day, or have we progressed beyond the need of repentance? What is the difference between repenting once for all and the need of a daily repentance?

6. How would you describe or characterize an apostate? When do men stand in the greatest danger of apostasy: in times of persecution or in times of easy living?

7. Compare once again the children of Israel in the wilderness and the Hebrew readers as the latter are portrayed in chapter 6.

8. Write on the thought, "crucify to themselves the Son of God afresh."

9. Is the sin spoken of in verses 4-8 the unpardonable sin? Who can commit that sin? Write a few sentences on your conception of that sin.

10. Describe the picture of a forerunner.

11. Who was Melchizedek? Why is he presented at the close of the chapter?

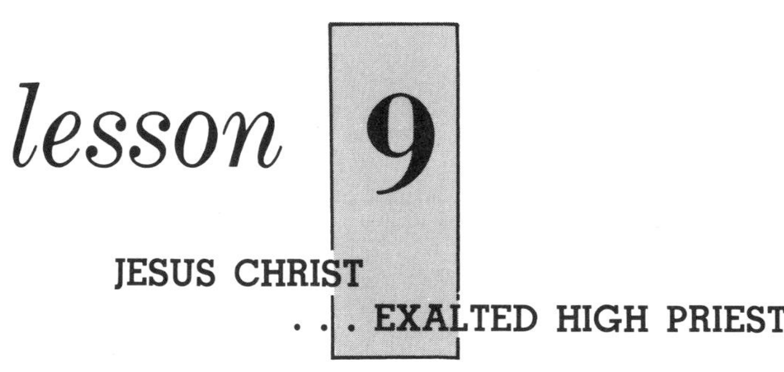

Hebrews 7

I. High priest after Melchizedek (vss. 1-11).

II. Eternal in His own right (vss. 12-19).

III. Verified by God's oath (vss. 20-21).

IV. Better priest in a better covenant (vss. 22-25).

V. Perfect in every priestly respect (vss. 26-28).

Chapter 7 opens with a detailed description of the greatness and superiority of Melchizedek as the Old Testament priest. After that description the question arises, "If he was so great, why is there need of another priest after his order?" The answer is that neither Melchizedek, nor Aaron, nor angels, nor Moses, nor any covenant, nor anything here on earth could satisfy God's demand as an atonement for sin, for everything was under the curse of sin (Rom. 3:23). It was essential that a sinless, eternal priest, the Lamb of God, the great high priest of chapter 4, come to offer the sacrifice God demanded and pay God's price of redemption. Melchizedek was a type of such an eternal priesthood realized in Jesus Christ.

Chapter 7 deals with a problem the readers faced: working out their salvation or better life by doing something. They thought that the better life was found in returning to Judaism and offering sacrifices according to the law of Moses and through the Aaronic priesthood. They judged this would make them acceptable to God, with the result that they would have peace and would be relieved of the pressure of possible persecution. On the contrary, states Hebrews, these Christians will bear pressures joyfully only because the peace they obtained came from the understanding, sinless, superior high priest — Jesus Christ.

This chapter shows Christ's superiority on these counts: (1) He is superior to Aaron because He is the eternal priest after Melchizedek's order; (2) He is an eternal priest according to God's oath, able to save to the uttermost because He came from heaven and is God's eternal Son; and (3) He is superior in that He offered sacrifices for sin once, so that will never again be necessary. This was in contrast to the continual stream of blood and constant sacrifices the Aaronic priesthood offered.

Chapter 7 consequently is cutting away the rationale and logic of these people wanting to go back to the Old Testament because the laws and practices were better. Here it is shown that the New Testament thinking and theology are absolutely necessary. In chapter 7 Jesus Christ is the one, only superior priest, the alpha and omega of God's plan of redemption. The writer is building up his case for changing from the Old to the New by demonstrating that Christ is *the great high priest.*

The change is from the whole Old Testament ritual and temple worship to a spiritual worship; from a continual flow of blood and a long succession of priestly sacrifices to the complete sacrifice of Jesus Christ — a once-and-for-all act.

Because Christ's priesthood is patterned after that of Melchizedek, we need to turn to the two references to Melchizedek in the Old Testament. The first is found in Genesis 14:8-20, with the heart of the matter being found in verses 17-20: "And the king of Sodom went out to meet him [Abraham], after his return from the slaughter of Chedorlaomer and the kings that were with him, at the vale of Shaveh (the same is 'the King's Vale'). And Melchizedek, king of Salem, brought forth bread and wine: and he was priest of God Most High. And he blessed him, and said, Blessed be Abram of God Most High . . . who hath delivered thine enemies into thy hand. And he gave him a tenth of all." The other reference to Melchizedek in the Old Testament is found in Psalm 110:4: "Jehovah hath sworn, and will not repent: Thou art a priest forever after the order of Melchizedek."

Much is made of Melchizedek. Some assert him to be the second Person of the Trinity incarnate in the Old Testament. They contend that he came in the flesh as an early theophany of the coming eternal high priest, Jesus Christ. Most likely not, for here the Bible may well be taken literally when it states, he "was *priest* of God Most High." He was not one of many priests nor was he even *the* priest of the Most High God, but he comes to us as priest to emphasize his work. Whether he was the only priest in Abraham's day or one of many, the Bible does not clarify. Nevertheless, before the day of a direct, specifically ordained priesthood (which came later through Aaron), Melchizedek is *priest*, that is, in general "for all men" he was priest of God.

In the day when God was to make the covenant of grace with Abraham and set aside Abraham and his descendants as His special people, we are introduced to the priestly work centered in this one man, Melchizedek. Before the Aaronic, specifically Israel-Judah priesthood, including tabernacle, sacrificial system, and even eventually temple worship and ritual, there was an antecedent, universal priest — Melchizedek. Even when the temple and the sacrificial order were instituted they were introduced with the apparent lesson that this was temporary until Christ came. Melchizedek's person and priesthood illustrated the eternal, spiritual priesthood of Christ, who not only followed in Abraham's line of covenantal relationship but also in Melchizedek's line of an eternal priesthood. Further, Christ's priesthood is typified not as a priesthood limited to one nation as that of Aaron's in Israel, but as a universal priesthood for all kindreds, nations, and tribes. For that reason Melchizedek is introduced as priest. It is not necessary, therefore, to think of Melchizedek as a theophany or appearance of the second Person of the Trinity, but rather as a man-priest.

A second truth taught by the Old Testament passage is that this man was not only priest, but also *king of Salem.* In other words, there were people living in Salem over whom this man was king and priest. The name Salem means "Peace." Melchizedek, therefore, was king of the city of peace. So Jesus Christ is also, by the words of the Old Testament and Hebrews, the King of Peace. The Scripture gives abundant evidence that Christ is our peace. Notice that the reference in Hebrews calls Melchizedek something else before naming him king of peace; it states "first being by interpretation King of righteousness, and after that also King of Salem." In reality, Christ had to be first of all our righteousness, our sacrifice for sin, before He could be our peace.

Abraham gives his tithe to a priest who also being king would bring peace and not war, for he was king of peace. Abraham had just completed a war and now at peace he also brings these tithes and offerings as a thanksgiving. Righteousness must be accomplished before there can be peace. Melchizedek therefore appears first as a priest, with the thought of sacrifice and offerings, and then as king, illustrating peace and quietness. Melchizedek as a type of the Lord Jesus Christ far exceeds the Aaronic type. Notice how prophecy is fulfilled in Christ's work when it first presents righteousness and then peace; for we read in Isaiah 32:17, "And the work of righteousness shall be peace; and the effect of righteousness, quietness and confidence for ever." Conceivably Abraham showed that he had fought a righteous war and now came bearing gifts of peace to the king of peace.

This thought is further sustained in those three "must" texts stated previously. In Hebrews 9:22 the Scripture posits that without the shedding of blood there is no remission of sin. Righteousness is obtained through the priestly work of Christ in the shedding of His blood. Hebrews 11:5, 6 demonstrates that this reality will not become individually meaningful until it is accepted by faith. Such Abraham demonstrated when he brought his tithes and offerings to Melchizedek. Later, in Hebrews 12:14, the peace idea is presented, for the text reads that we are to follow after "peace and righteousness" without which no man shall see God. The writer is consistently showing how Jesus Christ is the superior high priest, here in respect to righteousness and peace.

In Psalm 110 Christ is also portrayed as an eternal priest in these words, "Thou art a priest forever after the order of Melchizedek." The opening sentence of chapter 7 has as its main thought, "For this Melchizedek . . . abideth a priest continually." This priesthood is contrasted with Aaron's, which was purely temporal, made to last only as long as the Old Covenant, the law of the Old Testament, was in force. When the new dispensation came, the priesthood of Aaron was finished. It was a temporary thing, pointing ahead to a permanent reality, Jesus Christ, the great high priest.

In the light of the eternal, abiding priesthood of Jesus Christ, typified by Melchizedek, verse 3 reads, "without father, without mother, without genealogy, having neither beginning of days nor end of life, but made like unto the Son of God, abideth a priest continually." This important man appears on the pages of the Holy Bible in Genesis without any introduction. We are not told of his parents, when he was born, how old he was when he met Abraham; we do not know his ancestry, his economic standing in life, when he became a priest, nor when he died. Suddenly he is there and then he is gone; but the pages record him and because God's Word is a living Word he, too, lives on through the ages. In that way too he typifies Christ.

The verses that speak of Levi paying tithes to Melchizedek are significant. As universal humanity was represented in Adam's fall as the federal head of the race, so Abraham represented the covenantal people in this matter of paying tithes to Melchizedek. At the same time Levi and the priestly office of Aaron — all still in Abraham's loins — also were represented under Abraham as their head. Christ did not come from the line of Aaron but from Judah, with the result that Christ was not a priest according to the law of succession. He was not an Aaronic, temporal, sacrificing priest; but He was after the order of Melchizedek, the universal priest, eternal, righteous, and peace giving. In that He was superior to Aaron.

How does Melchizedek "abide a priest continually"? By the fact that in the Scriptures his successor is not mentioned. Was it his son? Who can tell? So — Melchizedek comes on the pages of the Bible as one lone figure. He has the center of attention; before him there is no one mentioned, after him no one is named successor. He stands alone — one priest living forever in the pages of the Word. In that light we must think of Christ after the order of Melchizedek.

Again, the Levitical priests received gifts or tithes from the Jews by law, but there was no law connected with the giving of tithes on the part of Abraham to Melchizedek. This was a voluntary sacrifice. There is a contrast between the Levitical system, which was a legal institution, and Melchizedek's priesthood, which was a free-will, out-of-love contribution. The Levitical priesthood did not secure perfection for it was part of the legal system, and the law showed how imperfect man was. The Levitical system had to be repeated constantly. Day after day and year after year sacrifices and offerings were given. There was a constant stream of blood of animals all through the ages until the precious blood of Jesus Christ was shed on Calvary. He alone was able to carry out the great sacrifice, and He was typified by the priesthood of Melchizedek.

The emphatic teaching of this chapter is that only in Jesus Christ would the Jews as well as the Gentiles — and we ourselves — find atonement and peace. The Jews could keep on going to the temple and sacrifice until the end of time, but they would never find true forgiveness and peace. That would only come through Jesus Christ.

The chapter concludes with the thought of a high priest who is "holy, guileless, undefiled, separated from sinners, and made higher than the heavens; who needeth not daily . . . to offer sacrifices . . . for this he did once for all, when he offered up himself." Christ voluntarily gave Himself as the one definitive sacrifice for our sins. That is the message of the chapter and the recurring theme of the book.

In summary, this chapter has presented Christ as high priest after the order of Melchizedek. That is:

1. He was priest from a different lineage than Aaron's; He was a universal priest.

2. He was, like Melchizedek, priest and king — priest of righteousness and king of peace.

3. He was priest of a covenant, chosen people, chosen throughout all the ages from all parts of the world irrespective of "color, race, or national origin," who through God's covenant of grace with Abraham had obtained righteousness. That is, they had been forgiven and had then voluntarily brought and would continually bring their gifts in peace to the king.

4. He is an eternal, ever-abiding, unchanging priest (vs. 24 and 13:8) who even now is in heaven making intercession for us.

5. The Levites still being in the loins of Abraham at the time that he offered gifts and sacrifices to Melchizedek indicates that the whole Levitical system offered sacrifices to the eternal system symbolized by Melchizedek. The Levitical service was inferior to the Melchizedek service as shown in the gifts the one brings to the other. In that picture too the Christ is portrayed as superior, in type receiving gifts through Melchizedek from the Levitical priesthood.

He is superior as a chief priest, as this chapter states in its closing words: "by the word of the oath, this Son is appointed perfect for evermore."

Personal reminders for:

1. Further study.

2. Further memorization.

3. Further Prayer.

Lesson 9

Questions, Topics, Suggestions for further study

1. What remedy did the Hebrew readers think would help them as they contemplated switching back to Judaism?

2. Write briefly on Melchizedek as a historical personage (Gen. 14); as a prophetic type (Ps. 110); and as a doctrinal, spiritual lesson and example (Heb. 7).

3. Give reasons as to whether or not you think Melchizedek was the second Person of the Trinity incarnate in the Old Testament.

   a.

   b.

4. Write on the meaning of the statement that Melchizedek was "priest," as a word that isn't prefixed by the term "the" or "a." How does this fit in with him as a type of Christ?

5. In what sense does Melchizedek remain "a priest continually"?

6. Why is Melchizedek first called "king of righteousness" and then "king of peace"?

7. What is the probable meaning of the fact that Melchizedek is listed as not having father or mother, neither genealogy?

8. Is there some significance to the fact that it was Abraham who brought gifts and offerings rather than Isaac, Jacob, or even Moses?

9. What is the central teaching of chapter 7?

10. Make a brief outline of the chapter in your own words. You may prefer to state what this chapter means to you or give some additional thoughts you have picked up in your reading or thinking.

11. Memorize at least two verses from this chapter (see vss. 25 and 26). It will be more beneficial for your study of this book if you will memorize some verses from each chapter.

lesson 10

THE TRIUMPHANT PRIEST
. . . MEDIATOR OF A BETTER COVENANT

Hebrews 8

I. Christ, the majestic high priest, is now seated victoriously in heaven (vs. 1).

II. He works continually as the mediator of a better covenant (vss. 2-7).

III. This covenant with His people is in their hearts (vss. 8-13).

    A. This covenant is living.

    B. This covenant assumes living knowledge of God.

    C. This covenant gives assurance of sins forgiven.

Although it may seem that the title above is mixing figures of thought, the fact is that Jesus Christ, having accomplished His earthly ministry of sacrificing for sin in obedience to the Father's will, went to heaven and sat down in triumph. He continues from heaven to give life to His covenant people by applying His sacrificial work of redemption to the hearts of His chosen ones.

The writer of this epistle makes that clear at the opening of chapter 8. He has been writing on a matter difficult to understand — the fact of Christ's priesthood patterned after that of Melchizedek's and not Aaron's. Now he sums up his teaching: "We have such a high priest, who sat down on the right hand of the throne of the Majesty in the heavens, a minister of the sanctuary, and of the true tabernacle, which the Lord pitched, not man" (vs. 1).

He is summing up several truths on which he had touched previously in order to keep the reader's mind on the fact that Jesus Christ is "better," "superior" to the Old Testament sacrificial and liturgical system. This is the summary:

1. We (New Testament Christians) also have a high priest just as the Old Testament believers had.

2. This high priest overcame sin, in fact, Himself paid the price of sin as is evidenced by the fact that —

    a. He triumphantly went to heaven and *sat down* (a proof of victory) at God's right hand.

    b. He is in majesty now as He was in humiliation here on earth.

    c. His ministry is a continual one.

d. He ministers in the true, abiding, eternal tabernacle made by the Lord and not by man's hands.

e. He is minister now of a better covenant because it is a living, eternal covenant obtained through His shed blood and placed in men's hearts by God Himself. As such a mediator and minister, He gives His subjects the better Christian life.

In chapter 8 we have reached the author's purpose for writing Hebrews. Here at almost mid-point we have his theme and conclusion in these words: "Now in the things which we are saying the chief point is this: We have such a high priest, who sat down on the right hand of the Majesty in the heavens" (8:1). The balance of the chapter illustrates and defines what he has stated and the conclusion to be drawn from that first verse is found in the last verse of the chapter: "In that he saith, a new covenant, he hath made the first old. But that which is becoming old and waxeth aged is nigh unto vanishing away" (8:13).

Chapter 8 deals with the mediatorial work of the Christ and the reason for it. The reason is that He has triumphed in His work on earth and now continues it as a victorious King in heaven. This ties in with Melchizedek who in chapter 7 was not only the king of righteousness (sacrifice, priest) but also king of Salem (peace). Consequently, Jesus Christ today functions as a victorious high priest, having paid the supreme sacrifice on Calvary in the shedding of His blood. But above all, He functions also as the triumphant King — King of peace (Rom. 5:1, 2).

This priest, Jesus Christ, is different. He is triumphant and is living eternally. For such a new Person, new rules of operation are needed. Therefore, after discussing the great high priest's difference, manifested particularly in this chapter through His work, the balance of the chapter is devoted to the new principles of operation, the new agreement, the covenant of which Jesus Christ because of His Person and work is the better head.

Another statement is needed to clear up an aspect of Christ's work contrasted with Aaron's. Every Old Testament priest worked for a short time of his life — just the best years. Every priest repeated his work year after year. Every priest had to be perfectly equipped for his work; he could have no blemish or spot. On every one of these counts, Jesus Christ was different. True, Christ carried out His earthly ministry in a brief period of time. But He was the eternal priest on the one hand — yet He performed His priestly function but once when He shed His blood on Calvary. True, He had no blemish. But He carried our sins and was condemned by law as guilty of death — yet He was actually not condemned or guilty, but in the eyes of the law He was tainted.

As to Christ's entrance into heaven, on that count He is superior, too. Year after year Aaron entered the Holy of Holies bearing the sins of the people. When he entered behind the veil because he was not perfect or sinless, he wasn't completely certain that the sins would be atoned for; he entered by faith and by anticipation that God would forgive. When Jesus Christ entered the heaven of heavens through the veil, He, in perfection, entered victoriously and triumphantly just once to take His seat at the right hand of God. He sat down — indicating victory over sin and obtainment of rest and peace now that the victory had been won. Even in that state of victory, peace and rest, He still works as the mediator of the new and living covenant.

When the chapter opens with the statement "we have such a high priest," what do we actually have?

1. God (Christ) who is "the effulgence of his glory, the very image of his substance . . . when he had made purification of sins" (1:3).
2. "A merciful and faithful high priest in things pertaining to God, to make propitiation for the sins of the people" (2:17).
3. He was a high priest who was "holy, guileless, undefiled, separated from sinners, and made higher than the heavens" (7:26).

This presentation of Christ throughout the book finally comes down to the basic truth that He is a *heavenly high priest,* confirmed in these words, "Now if he were on earth, he would not be a priest at all, seeing there are those who offer gifts according to the law; who serve that which is a copy and shadow of the heavenly things." This means that He is an eternal, perfect high priest dwelling in majesty.

We have then the picture that Christ was, in a factual, historical standpoint, no priest at all. He could have been that only after the order of Aaron; but He was not from the ancestry of Levi or Aaron, but rather from the line of David. While on earth, He did not perform any legally ordained priestly functions. His life was divided into the threefold work of preaching and teaching, performing signs and wonders, and example and conduct; but He never offered one sacrifice as priest. From one angle He acted as priest, that is in prayers and giving of Himself, but that was not according to the official sanction of the ordained priesthood in the temple. The official priesthood rejected Him, cast Him out of the temple and city, and finally it was the priests, Ananias and Caiaphas, who condemned Him to death.

But Christ was the priest in a spiritual sense, as a fulfillment of the type, for He offered Himself and at the same time was also the offering and the sacrifice. The point of the Scriptural reference is not to be taken that Christ's offering was merely exemplary, rather than sacrificial. The meaning is that if Christ were dwelling on earth as a human person, even as Aaron dwelt on earth, He would not be a priest as to His work and calling in life. He would be a carpenter or at best a teacher, but would not be in the priesthood. Yet He was also God and as God He filled the office of prophet, *priest,* and king.

In verses 1-6 two things are stated:

1. We have a high priest who through His ministry made atonement for us in His sacrifice.
2. We have a high priest who is a true minister of the true tabernacle, that is, the tabernacle in heaven.

Because of that latter reason God, in giving directions to Moses as to the building of the tabernacle, wanted him to follow to the last letter the divine specification. This tabernacle was to typify the eternal tabernacle in heaven. In order that men could have a picture of the heavenly tabernacle, God wanted Moses to build the type according to His heavenly blueprint. In building the earthly type God was using it as an object lesson to show how Jesus Christ would minister in the heavenly tabernacle as the superior high priest. Christ's priesthood therefore demonstrated this superiority because it is connected with the heavenly tabernacle and not with the earthly, which passed away, even as the earthly priest Aaron passed away.

In this section, therefore, we see that the superiority of the Lord Jesus Christ has a threefold emphasis. His is a better or "more excellent ministry" according to verse 6 and better promises are implied in verses 10 and 11.

1. Better ministry — because it is heavenly and not earthly, spiritual and not material.
2. Better covenant — because it is an absolute agreement with the Christian emphasis over against the Mosaic emphasis, which was conditional on Christ's coming. It was eternal and not temporal, being delivered once and for all to the saints. It was not limited to one nation but was universal. It was inner and not outward or external. It was vital in the heart and not external in a codified rule of conduct.
3. Better promises — because they are spiritual and eternal versus fleshly and temporal.

All the blessings then of this better ministry, better covenant, and better promises are obtained once and for all by the sacrificial work and heavenly ministry of the Lord Jesus Christ. Such a high priest we have; and for that we ought to be deeply grateful, for this is the foundation of the better Christian life.

From verses 7-13 the writer enlarges on the better covenant. This is one of the significant passages of the book, dealing with the covenant. The heart and essence of the book of Hebrews deals with the new covenant: its superiority and content as it relates to Jesus Christ, the great high priest.

A covenant or testament refers to a will made to be executed after one has died. This covenant became fully effective on the death of Christ. Technically a covenant is a contract or agreement between two parties, for the most part on equal terms, both capable of carrying out the contract as of the time it is made.

In the New Testament sense such cannot be the meaning; for this covenant is between God and man, and man is not equal to God, neither can he carry out any order of the covenant. It is only by God's grace that man can be considered a party to this covenant and is able to carry out its terms. God makes the covenant, specifies the terms, and then makes man the second party of the agreement. In addition, He gives him divine grace, enabling him to carry out the terms. The covenant reveals God's thinking regarding man and has as its purpose His glory through making man a partner with Him. Man consequently could have God's blessings and live in harmony and fellowship with Him. For this reason it is called the covenant of grace.

Why the New Covenant — The Covenant of Grace?

To that question verses 7 and 8 give the answer. The first legal covenant was imperfect in that it did not, in essence, do what it set out to do, in the sense of saving man. That was not the fault of the covenant, for "the law [or covenant] is holy and the commandment holy and righteous and good" (Rom. 7:12). The failure to meet the terms of that covenant is due to man's inability to keep it. Moreover, the covenant was temporary in the light of a new covenant to come. The Lord Himself, according to verse 8, stated that He would make a new covenant with the house of Israel. This showed that the old would pass away (Jer. 31:31-34).

Further, it is true that the covenant in itself was holy, blameless, and good; but it was imperfect in the sense that it did not finally gain salvation or peace or entrance into the heavenly sanctuary. That was due to the sinful nature of the people to whom it was given. As Erdman says, "God did not find fault with the covenant: but 'finding fault with them' He predicted the making of a new covenant" (*Hebrews*, p. 81).

Marks of the New Covenant

According to verse 10, it will be an *inner* covenant that is registered in the hearts and minds of people and will become a part of their living and thinking. This covenant will be a personal, family relationship; for God will be the God to those with whom He makes the covenant and they will be His children. It will be much more *intimate*, according to that picture. It will be an *intelligent* covenant, for verse 11 tells us that they will all know Him. "Intelligent" means that it isn't so many facts and commands given by God to be obeyed according to rote, but a knowledge that men have received, thought about, taken to heart; and because they know it is best, they willingly obey. It will be a covenant in which *iniquities are forgiven* because God is a merciful God. W. H. Griffith Thomas says in this connection that we have here represented "in the order of experience the four chief blessings of divine grace: (1) pardon; (2) fellowship; (3) consecration; (4) obedience. Thus the covenant as expressed in these terms may be regarded as the realization of the 'better promises' of verse six" (*Let Us Go On*, p. 105).

The last part of verse 13 reads, "But that which is becoming old and waxeth aged is nigh unto vanishing away." The old covenant and everything of it has vanished — it's through. God is finished with the old. Dispensationalists speak of a primary and secondary application — the former material, the latter spiritual; the former applying to Israel of the past with the possibility of a future manifestation of the former, the latter to the church. But such division of thought is not found here. There is but one living covenant — the covenant of grace, begun with Abraham in faith. Now that covenant, which is spiritual, is alive, present with and applying to a new people, the church of which Old Testament saints were also members by faith. This covenant with Christ's completed work ushers in, in a visible, living way the dispensation of God's sovereign grace and the kingdom of grace. To this grace there is no end. The contrast is between a covenant of law and works and a covenant of grace and faith.

The explanation of this chapter ends on a note of victory. The old has passed away forever and now the covenant of grace, in which all are included who come by humble faith through grace in Christ, is active and in force. As recipients of that covenant of grace, Christians truly have better living through Christ.

The weakness of the Old Covenant is seen in the light of what the New Covenant promises in meeting man's deepest needs.

1. In promising forgiveness of sin through Jesus Christ, the New Covenant meets man's need for cleansing, for companionship, and for consecration. The Old Covenant never gave a sense of completion, or of satisfaction, since it made continual and continuing demands.
2. In promising an inner power, the New Covenant gives the newly saved man strength to overcome his weaknesses in his journey toward holiness on the road of sanctification.
3. In promising identity and unity with Christ in the New Covenant, the possession of security is assured.
4. In promising union in the New Covenant, God guarantees a fuller and deeper revelation of Himself as He dwells in intimate fellowship with the believer.

When God and man have been restored to fellowship, these are the benefits:

1. Our sins are not only forgiven but forgotten.
2. We shall be striving for the higher things. Instead of seeking to *know ourselves*, we shall strive to *know God;* and as we seek Him we shall learn to know ourselves and our world better.

   It is a matter of basic philosophy that if our chief aim is to live for self all striving will be geared to that end. When God takes over in our lives we will strive to live in a way that is pleasing to Him. It is in that light the Scriptures speak of a time when "they shall not teach every man his fellow-citizen, and every man his brother, saying, Know the Lord" (Heb. 8:11). All will be living and working to "know the Lord," and knowing Him and having experienced His love all will strive to perfect their walk with Him.
3. The above truths give us the assurance and reality of abiding fellowship with Christ.
4. As a result we are consecrated to loving and serving Him.
5. We give Him our unadulterated, voluntary obedience, born not from any legal demands but flowing out of the love of our heart.

Lesson 10
Questions, Topics, Suggestions for further study

1. Chapter 8 deals with what aspects of Christ's superiority?

2. Discuss the view that Christ is now a high priest in heaven.

3. Give the three thoughts under "having such a high priest."

   a.

   b.

   c.

4. In what sense was Christ not a priest?

5. What two things do verses 1-6 teach us?

   a.

   b.

6. Why did God give such specific directions to Moses for the building of the tabernacle?

7. Name the threefold superiority of Christ as brought out in this
chapter.

   a.

   b.

   c.

8. Define "covenant." In what sense does this definition fall short
when we deal with Scriptural covenants?

9. Why was the new covenant necessary?

10. Give the marks of the new covenant.

    a.

    b.

    c.

    d.

11. What does verse 13 tell of the passing of that which is old?

12. What is the theme of the book as stated in this chapter? Write it
and memorize it.

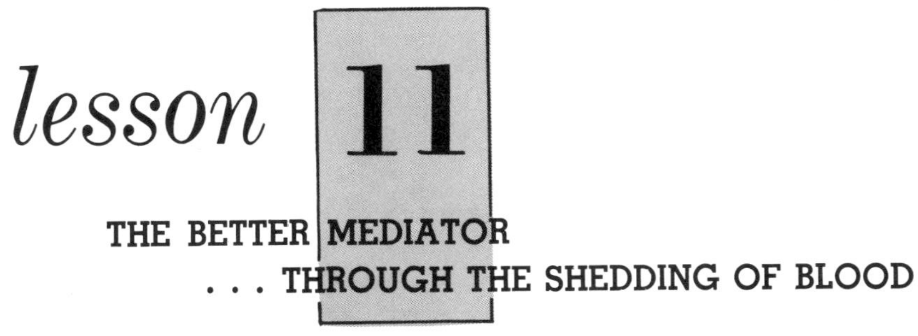

lesson 11

THE BETTER MEDIATOR
. . . THROUGH THE SHEDDING OF BLOOD

Hebrews 9

I. The first covenant's ordinances listed (vss. 1-5).

II. The work carried on by the first covenant (vss. 6-10).

III. Christ, the high priest of good things to come (vss. 11-14).

IV. Christ, the mediator of the better covenant through the shedding of blood (vss. 15-22).

V. Christ, the "once for all" sacrifice for sin (vss. 23-28).

The topic under discussion, which was carried over from chapter 8, is *the covenant*. The writer has been proving the superiority of the new covenant over the Old Testament. Up to this point we have seen that the old covenant was not faultless (in no way was it to blame, however, for the failure that resulted from it), since it did not succeed in having its members keep it. Further, there were better promises that came from the second covenant. Those better promises described in chapter 8 were:

1. The law would be internal, written on the heart.
2. God would be known universally rather than by a specific group, the Jews, or even more specifically, the priests and prophets.
3. God would through the new covenant, that is, through Christ, forgive our sins and we would be brought into fellowship with Him.
4. Because of the blessings of the new covenant, we would know Him and love Him.

We think of the new covenant in terms of God's gracious agreement with Abraham and therefore speak of it as the covenant of grace. This covenant then came to its full manifestation in the Lord Jesus Christ. Hebrews, however, does not speak of the covenant in that exact way. In fact it makes no reference to Abraham, as the Apostle Paul does particularly in Galatians. Hebrews does speak of promises to Abraham, however, but not in covenantal terms (6:13; 7:6).

The Covenant Described

Covenantal theology is important and because we get an exposition of it in chapters 8 and 9, we need to examine the teaching of the covenant more closely.

In the covenant of grace, God above all takes the initiative and it is He who really is all in all. For matters of definition and understanding it can be explained in this way: *The covenant of grace is that gracious agreement between an offended, loving, merciful God and the offending sinner who, though lost in sin, is yet chosen of God. In that agreement God out of pure grace promises salvation full and free through faith in Christ; and the sinner, on no merits of his own but out of sovereign grace, accepts this promise in faith. This promise of God gives him eternal life; and for that, by grace again, he promises a life of faith and obedience to his covenant God.* In that loving bond of fellowship, the covenant child lives the better Christian life.

The covenant is not an end in itself but a means looking toward an end: that of bringing its members to a mature, living relation of mutual agreement and cooperation in Christ. The fact is that because of sin there was estrangement, and so the covenantal agreement makes estranged parties harmonious again. Sin does not automatically vanish by virtue of a person's being in the covenant, even though the covenant we are dealing with is the covenant of grace. Grace and faith, together with prayer, need to stay active for the realization of the promises of the covenant, including constant forgiveness of sins.

In the Old Testament the sin was typically removed by the whole sacrificial system. In the New Testament and in our day once our sin is gone, sins of wilful deeds and sins of omission are also removed by the precious blood of Jesus Christ through our constant prayer to Him for forgiveness. This new covenant is written in our hearts so that they become alive, hearts of flesh instead of stone (8:10). Our thinking and will, however, in spite of that may sin wilfully (10:26). Therefore we have to "hold fast" and be frequently "at the throne of grace." Even though we have been forgiven and the estrangement is gone, we need the continuing assurance of God's grace in seeking daily forgiveness.

This letter to the Hebrews then goes on to show at some length the failure of the old covenant and the superiority of the new. The reason for its superiority is the Person and work of Jesus Christ, "the mediator of a better covenant."

As we now come more specifically to an exposition of chapter 9, we see that it contrasts the old covenant with the new and reaches its climax in verses 11 and 12: "But Christ having come a high priest of the good things to come, through the greater and more perfect tabernacle, not made with hands, that is to say, not of this creation, nor yet through the blood of goats and calves, but through his own blood, entered in once for all into the holy place, having obtained eternal redemption."*

---

*In studying the significance of the blood, one should realize that the blood first of all had to do with God. It was God's demand of His Son and it was because of the agreement between the Father and the Son, that the Son would and did shed His blood as the payment God demanded for our redemption. When this had been done, then the blood became meaningful for us. In that light, study these texts:

1. "Unto him that loveth us, and loosed us from our sins by his blood" (Rev. 1:5b).
2. "For thou wast slain, and didst purchase unto God with thy blood men of every tribe" (Rev. 5:9).
3. "And through him to reconcile all things unto himself, having made peace through the blood of his cross" (Col. 1:20).
4. "And he said to me, These are they that come out of the great tribulation, and they washed their robes, and made them white in the blood of the Lamb" (Rev. 7:14).

Look at the contrast and comparison between the old and new covenants:

THE OLD COVENANT

(Here called the "first covenant")
This covenant had:
1. Ordinances of divine service.
2. A sanctuary of this world.
3. A prepared tabernacle in which were:
   a. The candlestick
   b. The table — in the Holy Place
   c. The showbread
4. The Holy of Holies.
   a. A golden altar of incense (actually not in the Holy of Holies, but rather *belonging to* or *pertaining to* the Holy of Holies; cf. I Kings 6:22).
   b. Ark of the covenant.
      (1) Golden pot of manna.
      (2) Aaron's budding rod.
      (3) Tables of the covenant.
      (4) Cherubims of glory overshadowing the mercy-seat.
5. Priests who went into the Holy Place.
6. The high priest who entered the Holy of Holies.
7. Blood of offerings and gifts brought into this tabernacle.

THE NEW COVENANT

(Here called the "second covenant")
This covenant had:

1. Christ, as high priest of the good things to come.

2. The greater and more perfect tabernacle not made with hands.

3. Christ's own blood, cleansing our consciences from dead works.

4. Eternal redemption.

In this part of chapter 9 we are dealing with the service rendered by the two covenants. The first rendered a detailed service, for it had a tabernacle (rather than the temple — which did come later) to show its temporary character — with all of its equipment. It further had the ministers, that is, the priests who rendered the services. Also it had the materials with which to render service: the calves, the goats, the water, and all that was needed to do the work effectively. The second covenant had the Person of Jesus Christ, the high priest after the order of Melchizedek. It had His blood and an eternal tabernacle not made with hands. From outward show, the former might have seemed better; but in actual content, the latter was far superior.

The old can be summarized in the thought of incompleteness and inadequacy as the chapter itself states, "The Holy Spirit thus signifying that the way into the holy place hath not yet been made manifest, while the first tabernacle is yet standing." The blood of goats and bulls and calves was typical of incompleteness, the whole thing pointing to the coming of the Lord Jesus Christ.

Christ, the Better Mediator of a Better Covenant

Beginning with verse 11, the author is concentrating on the better aspects of the mediator. Christ, the better mediator —

1. Is a better priest (vs. 11).
2. Dwells in a better tabernacle (vs. 11).
3. Offers a better blood, His own (vs. 12).
4. Accomplishes a better work, "once for all" (vs. 12).
5. Obtains a better redemption, "eternal" (vs. 12).
6. Gives a better cleansing, "cleanse your conscience from dead works" (vss. 13, 14).
7. Is mediator of a new, "living covenant" (vss. 15, 19).
8. Is the purifier of sin, "through the shedding of blood" (vss. 20-22).

The contents of verses 14-22 deals with the atoning death of Christ in which He shed His blood to secure the promises of this better covenant. Christ made this sacrifice as the great high priest and in so doing abolished sin. This is spelled out in these words: "And for this cause he is the mediator of a new covenant, that a death having taken place for the redemption of the trangressions that were under the first covenant, they that have been called may receive the promise of the eternal inheritance" (vs. 15).

Here then is the picture of the unity of the Old and the New Testament. In a sense the sins of the Old Testament saints were really not done away with until Jesus Christ cried out on the cross, "It is finished." Of course they were saved, but it was a salvation based on the anticipated actual accomplishment of Christ on the cross. Faith was essential in the Old Testament, too — faith in the ability of the promised Messiah to save those who by faith anticipated His coming.

There is also an argument present for the necessity of Christ's death. The covenant would never have been effected if Christ had not died. The writer at this point wishes to show that Christ's death and shedding of blood were necessary to secure what the covenant promised. When He died, the terms of the covenant were actually realized. By His death the saints — past, present, and future — had salvation effectually guaranteed and given them. Consequently, without the shedding of that blood of Christ there would have been no will or covenant of His in force; and so the writer states that "apart from the shedding of blood there is no remission" of sin.

The third division of the chapter is from verses 23-28. Here the author is showing two things: (1) the shedding of Christ's blood took away sin and confirmed the covenant; and (2) Christ entered into heaven to appear before the face of God to show Him the completed work. Because of those accomplishments He will some time return to take us with Him in glory to dwell before the throne of God.

In verses 23-28 we have three appearings of Christ. They are really past, present, and future.

1. "He hath been manifested to put away sin" (vs. 26).

2. "But into heaven itself, now to appear" (vs. 24).

3. "Shall appear a second time . . . unto salvation" (vs. 28).

To restate those three thoughts: each appearance had a specific purpose. The first time Christ was manifested in connection with sin to put it away by living in constant humiliation and by His sacrifice on the cross. After that He entered heaven to present that victory to God and from that time on to act as our advocate, mediator, and intercessor. Finally the future appearance will be in power and great glory as our King, to take us unto Himself to reign with Him forever.

❊   ❊   ❊   ❊

VERSES TO MEMORIZE

HEBREWS

Lesson 11

Questions, Topics, Suggestions for further study

1. Give a résumé of the better promises of the new covenant.

2. Show that a covenant is a means to an end.

3. Define the covenant of grace in your own words. Try to get a brief definition you can easily memorize.

4. Does being in the covenant of grace mean that such a person will never again sin? Give reasons for your answer.

5. Contrast the old covenant with the new covenant.

6. What services do the covenants presented in this chapter render?

7. Why was the old covenant inadequate?

8. Give five ways in which Christ and the new covenant are superior
to the Old Testament.

a.

b.

c.

d.

e.

9. Why was it necessary for Christ to die as to the fulfillment of the
covenant of grace?

10. In what three senses does this chapter speak of Christ's appearing?

a.

b.

c.

lesson 12

CHRIST, THE SUPREME SACRIFICE
. . . OUR ONLY HOPE

Hebrews 10

I. The old sacrifices were not sufficient to atone for sin (vss. 1-4).

II. Christ's sacrifice alone satisfies (vss. 5-10).

III. Proofs of Christ's superior sacrifice (vss. 11-18).

IV. Exhortations to accept the benefits of Christ's sacrifice (vss. 19-25).

V. Vengeance on those who scorn His sacrifice (vss. 26-31).

VI. Remember former blessed days as incentives to godly living (vss. 32-39).

The first half of the chapter (vss. 1-18) offers the concluding argument in the general thesis that Jesus Christ is the better sacrifice and high priest. This section has two parts, the first comprising verses 1-10 which ends with these words, "By which will we have been sanctified through the offering of the body of Jesus Christ *once for all.*" The purpose is to show the definitive character of the one, specific, all-sufficient sacrifice of Jesus Christ.

The second part, verses 11-18, shows that Christ's sacrifice causes God to remember our sins no more for there has been remission of sin by the shedding of His blood. There is therefore no more need for the shedding of blood. The emphatic word there is "final," or as the Hebrew writer puts it: "once." At this point "once" deals with the completeness of Christ, the divine-human sacrifice, over against the animal sacrifices of the Old Testament. Further, Christ appeased God with His sacrifice, contrasted to the blood of bulls and goats which satisfied God only because they were typifying Christ's coming. Those old sacrifices, however, if not offered in faith were not at all pleasing to Him. As Psalm 40:6 states, "Sacrifice and offering thou wouldest not."

As noted, there is a contrast between animal sacrifice as a typical atonement for sin and Jesus Christ, as actual atonement. One wonders if Jesus Christ Himself ever offered sacrifices. The answer could be negative, for why should He? He was not a sinner, yet the other side is seen in the question of paying tribute when Peter was asked whether tribute had been paid to the authorities. The order Christ gave Peter implies that the sons of the king needed to pay no tribute; but Jesus did pay, obtaining the coin from the mouth of the fish and giving the tribute through Peter. This was not compulsory, though; for He was the King and the heavens and the earth belonged to Him. One must consider, however, that He was obedient in all things and as such He was baptized as under the law. To fulfill all righteousness He possibly also sacrificed as obeying the law, but not as an atonement for His sins, for He had none, but for ours.

Jesus Himself adds further light on this matter of performing the demands of the law when He stated just before His baptism, "Suffer it now: for thus it becometh us to fulfill all righteousness" (Matt. 3:15).

The first idea in this chapter is that one can continue the sacrifices of the Old Testament indefinitely without ever obtaining the forgiveness of sin. Over against that, Jesus Christ was offered once; and that one sacrifice was sufficient to remove sin forever. In carrying out this sacrifice, Jesus Christ was doing the will of the Father and was well pleasing to Him.

From verses 11-18 another thought is advanced. The contrast in those verses is between the priest standing day by day ministering and offering sacrifices — showing the incomplete character of this work — and Jesus Christ who, having offered one sacrifice, completed the work and sat down at the right hand of the Father. He remains there until His enemies will have been subdued. There was no furniture in the temple for sitting; one stood. The heavenly scene is a throne on which one sat, indicating rest or completed work, because of an accomplished task.

In these verses we see the superiority of Christ's sacrifice on two more counts: (1) His triumphant sitting at the right hand of God; (2) His perfecting or sanctifying forever those for whom He died. This the Old Testament priest and sacrifices could never do. That such is true and that Christ is superior is brought out by the testimony and work of the Holy Spirit in applying to the heart of the believer that which Christ had obtained. The writer has proved his case of Christ's superiority when he completed verse 18.

The conclusion to this part of the chapter is that the old covenant was a shadow; the new, complete, fulfillment. The old signified incompletion; the new, completion. The old kept men in bondage continually; the new gave freedom. The old passed away; the new remains eternal. The old kept men everlastingly sacrificing; the new gave remission of sin through the blood of Christ, once for all. Sacrifice for sin is over.

In verses 19-39 we have the application of the previous teachings. We have the applications which follow from the fact that Jesus Christ is the superior high priest and sacrifice; and we have warnings which must be heeded because we deal with such a wonderful high priest and sacrifice, Jesus Christ.

Verses 19-25 may be divided as follows: The Christian is inspired to —
1. Boldness through the blood.
2. Draw near through faith.
3. Hold fast the confession of hope.
4. Consider to good works.
5. Assemble and exhort because of the approaching end.

The first thought of this section (reminding us of chapter 4:14-16) is that we should possess confidence to enter through our prayers into the heavenly habitation where Christ is. We would have fears, but our hearts are strong in faith and our consciences clean through our high priest. For a man to approach God with confidence is a new thing, something Christ accomplished by coming in the flesh, shedding His blood and entering into the Holy of Holies within the veil, that is, entering heaven. Going through the veil of the temple was the only means by which a priest could enter the Holy of Holies. In the same manner, it is only because of the piercing of the body of our Savior, the shedding of His blood, His penetration of the clouds and His entering heaven, that we can enter the Holy of Holies.

In this section we have the work resting on us in the light of what Christ has accomplished. It is a threefold work reaching out to God, holding fast ourselves in the faith, and demonstrating the love of God in us by provoking ourselves to good works. Here is the practical application of Matthew 22:37-40. This is the New Testament application of Christ's love for us in our response to God and our neighbor.

We are urged to draw near. As of today we draw near in prayer; at some future time our soul will draw near into heaven when it separates from the body; and lastly the body will draw near when it is reunited with the soul in the resurrection.

In this passage there are three of the "let us" references. These are:

1. "Let us draw near with a true heart in fullness of faith" (vs. 22).
2. "Let us hold fast the confession of our hope" (vs. 23).
3. "Let us consider one another to provoke unto love and good works" (vs. 24).

These "let us" passages are offered in view of the dangers that are rampant. The dangers are of —

1. Wavering (vs. 23).
2. Forsaking the assembling together (vs. 25).
3. Falling away.

In verses 26-31 we have another series of warnings similar to the ones in chapter 6, dealing with apostasy. The warnings are given in the light of the exhortations and dangers mentioned above. Such apostasy as gleaned from this passage can overtake two classes of people, but we often limit it to the first class. The first group are those who sin wilfully. That is plainly stated; but another class is implied and those are the ones who just drift, or those who forsake the assembling of themselves with the saints, or those who fail to draw near and will end as apostates. These slowly, gradually, yet just as definitely forsake the Lord Jesus Christ and become the objects of God's wrath as do those who act boldly and wilfully. They, too, are negating the commandments of God and are just as truly crushing them underfoot as are the wilful sinners.

The persons written about in these verses have done the following acts that indicate they are apostate and do not care for the eternal realities:

1. They had trodden under foot the Son of God (vs. 29).

2. They had counted the blood of the covenant as an unholy thing (vs. 29).
3. They had done despite to the Spirit of grace (vs. 29).

The greatness of the sin is indicated in their despising the great sacrifice or work of Jesus Christ, the superior high priest, just as in chapter 6 the sin was against the eternal Holy Spirit who was working in the hearts of the believers, showing them the wonderful Person, Jesus Christ. Here the sin, which in chapter 6 was a sin against the Person, is against the work of Christ. In chapter 6 the sin is against the divinity of the Person; here it is against the efficacy of His work, for there is a rejecting of His vicarious, atoning, bloody sacrifice offered once for all. The picture from the original is that this is not just one blatant outburst of sin, but it is a continual thing. It is a habit with those who live this way. These people, whether they do so wilfully in a deliberate, well-thought-out and defined position or whether they just go along, are still doing so by choice and with a deliberate decision. What is the outlook for these wilful sinners? Terrible indeed is their end. There is —

1. No more a sacrifice for sins (vs. 26).
2. A fearful expectation of judgment (vs. 27).
3. A fierceness of fire (vs. 27).
4. A terrible possibility of falling into the hands of the living God who is a consuming fire (vs. 31).

Such persons have turned traitor to the Lord Jesus Christ and become the worst archfiends that Christ or Christianity could have. They do the most damage to the Christian program and cannot experience God's mercy. They have despised God's Person and work, so by their choice there can be no mercy. They are the ones who do not want it and who deliberately cast it aside. These are religious quislings and fifth columnists of the highest order — traitors indeed.

Consider for a moment God's vengeance. There are those today who think and write only about God in terms of love. Such He is, but in order for Him to be that, there must be another side. God is a God of vengeance. He demonstrated that in the Old Testament. Think of the condemnation of the Israelites to forty years of desert wanderings. Think of Moses being chastised by not entering the promised land. Think of His judgment of Korah, Dathan, and Abiram. All these illustrations are taken from God's people, Israel, with whom God had special dealings. To reject and discount God and His covenant is to despise the living God. God indeed lives and as the living God He will bring His wrath and vengeance to bear on these despisers. These apostates fall into the hands of this living God. Indeed "God is slow to anger and plenteous in love"; but once His anger has been aroused, woe to those who fall into His hands.

This writer must have been a kind man, for after having written the terrible things he comes back with words of assurance. In the final analysis, however, these are not only a kind man's words but God's words; and God is a kind God. After showing the terribleness of His wrath, a wrath that falls on man because of his own sin and wilfulness,

God does not wish any to be hopeless or despairing or to perish. Therefore He comes with a message of hope.

Passages like the above and the one in chapter 6 may cause earnest Christians deep trouble. The devil likes to afflict them and cause them to worry; yet God watches over and tenderly loves His children. True, we do sin and for a time may even backslide; but God still loves us and we still love Him and we shall come back to Him and love Him even more, provided we are His legitimate, born-again children. From verses 32 to the end of the chapter, the writer is assuring those who do believe in Jesus Christ, who do love their Lord and who might be terrified by the threatened judgment with its terrible consequence, that such words do not apply to them because "we are not of them that shrink back" (vs. 39). He sets out to prove this by recalling the former days in which —

1. They were enlightened (vs. 32).
2. They endured a great conflict of sufferings by being made a gazing stock both by reproaches and afflictions and by themselves suffering along with those ill treated (vss. 32, 33).
3. They took compassion on the persecuted ones and had their possessions spoiled for the sake of the persecuted ones (vs. 34).

If they went back through memory's lane they could recall these testings; and to recall them was to give them comfort, for they had come through successfully. Such memory ought to give them confidence for the future. This being true, the potentialities of holding steadfast were a present reality; but great patience was needed. And then Habakkuk 2:3 and 4 are quoted to indicate that the promise would soon be fulfilled for them and that the promised One would come. This was fulfilled in Christ who did come and who does help. The justified children therefore should live in and by faith. That is the only way a righteous man can live, since God has no pleasure in any man that draws back.

The chapter ends with this reassuring statement, "But we are not of them that shrink back unto perdition; but of them that have faith unto the saving of the soul."

ADDED STUDIES ON THE HOLY SPIRIT'S WORK IN THE BOOK OF HEBREWS

HEBREWS

Lesson 12

Questions, Topics, Suggestions for further study

1. Give the various teachings of each section in chapter 10.

2. Why were the sacrifices of the Old Testament continuously needed? Why did they ultimately prove to be futile?

3. Show the contrast between the priest *standing* in the tabernacle or temple and Jesus Christ *sitting* at the Father's right hand.

4. Name four lessons the Christians are to learn in verses 19-25.

   a.

   b.

   c.

   d.

5. What dangers are warned against in this section?

6. Explain the meaning of verses 26-31 in terms of falling away from
   Christianity. Can a true Christian ever really fall away?

7. What does the apostate do that makes him fall away? At least
   three things are given.

   a.

   b.

   c.

8. Once a person becomes apostate, what four terrible things are true?

   a.

   b.

   c.

   d.

9. Why is God a God of vengeance and wrath? Show that He is also
   a God of love.

10. Why would the true Christians never fall away as apostates?

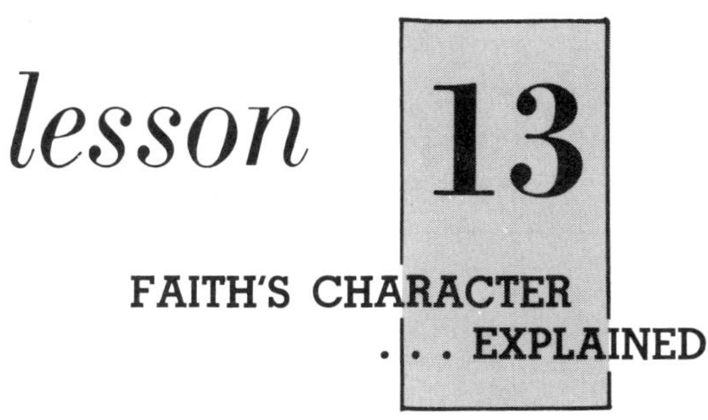

FAITH'S CHARACTER
. . . EXPLAINED

Hebrews 11 (I)

I. Faith explained (vss. 1-3).

II. Faith illustrated (vss. 4-12).

III. Faith maintained (vss. 13-16).

IV. Faith tried (vss. 17-31).

V. Faith defended (vss. 32-40).

In chapter 11 the Holy Spirit has a concentrated study on several aspects of faith as it pertains to the Christian life, the purpose being to show that the man of faith will be able to live the Christian life in the midst of a hostile world. This chapter demonstrates how faith makes the Christian live the better Christian life through Christ, the better mediator.

The Holy Spirit also in other passages has concentrated teachings on subjects needing emphasis because of problems that bother readers, as the problem of remaining true to the faith bothered the readers here. Illustrations are found in I Corinthians 13 on love, I Thessalonians 4 on the certainty of Christ's return, and Romans 8 on the teaching of the Person and work of the Holy Spirit. Such in-depth, concentrated teachings scattered throughout the Bible are helpful to the reader and student.

The author of Hebrews has been building up to and preparing his readers for this chapter on faith. In chapter 10 the writer quoted an Old Testament passage (Hab. 2:3, 4), which deals with faith, to encourage and help those who were being tempted to backslide. In this chapter there is an enlarging on the theme of faith and an exposition as an illustration that the Old Testament saints also were sustained and saved by faith. Faith is essential to the existence of spiritual life, the absolute necessity for the Christian. In the light of that context, including chapter 10, chapter 11 is written. In fact, W. H. Griffith Thomas on page 140 of *Let Us Go On* brings out that chapter 10:22-25 records encouragements or exhortations to hold on to and to increase in faith (vs. 22), hope (vs. 23), and love (vs. 24). The writer of Hebrews then proceeds to enlarge on those three concepts, writing on faith in chapter 11, hope in chapter 12, and love in chapter 13.

Various and glamorous titles have headed this chapter on faith. Some have said that the passage deals with *The Heroes of Faith,* and it does. Others have called it *God's Honor Roll of Faith,* and what an honor it is to be listed. This is God's honor roll, for man would never think of putting such individuals as Samson and Jephthah in the list. One could even call this list *The Galaxy of God's Spiritual Warriors.* Its title could read: *Faith's Who's Who,* and then would be listed the names and accomplishments of the faithful followers of God throughout the Old Testament period. But such titles are not found in the Scripture. God Himself gave the contents of the chapter without titles. He did so to prove that His gift of faith keeps men in all ages and under all conditions safe from apostasy. Faith alone will enable the believer to overcome the danger of falling away.

In the opening of the chapter, there is no theological definition of faith, but an explanation of what it is. The emphatic thought of the writer comes down to this: Faith *is* right now an assurance of things hoped for, a conviction right now of things not seen. Faith gives meaning, body, and content right now to realities that many persons think are future uncertainties. Because of the intangible aspects of the Christian life, many were unable and unwilling to suffer in the present for the sake of the future fulfillment of promised eternal joy.

This chapter illustrates that even the Old Testament saints, who in their day did not have the fulfillment of the promise, did endure. Faith has reality at all times, for it is certain (tried, tested) knowledge and a hearty assurance now of the eternal truth still not seen with the naked eye.

In looking at this concept of faith several thoughts need to be borne in mind. First there must be an object for faith. That object is a statement or a promise, or an actual body of facts. Then there must be some type of confidence in one's own ability to believe. Third, there must be an assurance that both the object of faith and the subject — the person believing in this mutual exercise — will realize the fulfillment of that which is believed. In other words, the subject expects that the facts in which he has placed confidence will turn out to be as true in the future as he thinks them to be at the time he places his assurance in them.

In the opening verses of the chapter the writer is assuring his readers that the unseen realities in which they have confidence are just as real — in fact, even more real — than the things which can be seen, heard, or felt. The reason is that oftentimes the visible, tangible things are not what they seem to be. Since these unseen realities are assured and given of God, they are "yea and amen," for God is real and true and so are the things He gives. The faith aspect here is one of action; faith is not passive but active. It goes out to; it lays hold of; it rests on someone or something. That something is the Word of God and that someone is God. God has spoken and in His speaking has made promises. These promises the believer takes as real.

In a sense we have here an emphasis on what faith is able to do, in that it makes the unseen to be seen and the future to be present. Isn't that the whole point in enumerating a long line of heroes from the Old Testament who lived and died in the light of seeing what others did not see and realizing in their life what others thought was impossible? Isn't this the mark of the leaders? They have visions that are real to them and they translate these dreams into living deeds. Faith in the religious sphere leads men to say, "I have been to the mountain top; I have caught a vision of the promised land." It leads men to sing again today the words of that Civil War hymn, "Mine eyes have seen the glory of the coming of the Lord." In Christianity, these visions are borne of God who gives men the spiritual insight by faith to see their eternal realities.

The first three verses of the chapter are an exposition of the character of faith. The author brings out that through faith, those who believed lived securely, placing confidence in the word and promises of God. Men needed answers to the problems they met in their life and world, and they found them in God in whom they believed. That solved for them their basic questions and persistent riddles.

For instance, the opening verses speak of the origin of the universe. No one saw it made, no one was present at its beginning, but it's here; therefore, how did it get here? The Christian believes that "the worlds were framed by the word of God." That answer gives unity and purpose to the seen world. Yet how does one know that this faith is right? The answer is in the word "understand," which has in it the thought of divine revelation. Somehow through the operation of the Holy Spirit, the Christian grasps by faith that this is right. God gave a revelation — look at His world and Word — and this revelation man by faith accepts as true, that is, that God is the author of this world. In other words, God in His act of creation is speaking to man; and man accepts this work and word of God by faith. The reasonableness of this declaration of Scripture is borne out by the fact that as man accepts, he has the key that unlocks the problem of the universe's existence. This is the consistent, unified teaching of Scripture.

But faith is not something only in one's heart; it comes out in one's life. In fact, that is the contention of chapter 11 for the writer says, "for therein the elders had witness borne to them." In proving that statement, the author presents elder after elder who had witness borne to them, and as a result faith in God enabled these elders to overcome the world. Now that "witness borne" is a conviction that is God given. In reality it is a power by which God enables them to see the unseen and to believe what otherwise would be impossible to believe. That power caused them to act as they did.

That is equally true today. The Christian says he believes that God made the world, over against a naturalistic philosophy which says that such is impossible. The Christian because of faith preaches the gospel, which to the world is foolishness. These elders in the chapter had a power through faith that enabled them to be persecuted, ill treated, tormented for the sake of the kingdom of God. That same power lives in the Christian believer today. This matter of faith was not then and is not now sentiment, or emotion, or feeling (although all of these are included), but solid evidence from God. Believing is just as real as acting; it is not a whim of fancy or a wave of feeling. It is substance, solid and real, given by God.

The writer goes back to the beginning, to creation, and tells us we shall have to believe that the world comes from God's hands. That is basic to the understanding of God's dealing all through the ages. From that point he proceeds with the characters from the dawn of history to the time when the epistle was written. He is tracing through human history the past reality of faith — how it enabled men to live and die successfully. After speaking about the creation of the world, which we understand to come from God's hand, he shows how with that kind of faith, which believes in God, Abel offered a better sacrifice than Cain.

Here is another point of superiority. Faith enables men to lead superior lives, and that faith — incidentally even in that Old Testament time — is faith in the coming mediator. Because Abel had faith in God, he was acceptable to God. Actually, he himself was acceptable and that made the deeds of his hands acceptable. His deeds, which declared his complete belief in God, were an expression of his heart. The writer tells us that Abel offered a better sacrifice than Cain. In the story in Genesis we are not told why it was better; but here, centuries later, we find out and the answer is that Abel offered in faith. He saw the unseen while Cain did not.

Before proceeding, here is a composite picture of the different things faith is and does as it is presented in chapter 11:

1. "Faith is that which enables us to treat as real the things that are unseen."
2. "Faith is the ground of things hoped for, that is, trust in God, or the conviction that God is sovereign and good and that He will perform His promises."
3. "Substantially the words mean that faith gives to things future, which as yet are only hoped for, all the reality of actual present existence." (These quotations are taken from *The Expositor's Greek Testament*, Vol. 4, p. 352.) These elements of faith were verified in the lives of the heroes of faith mentioned in this chapter.

This brings us again to the first hero mentioned in chapter 11, Abel. Abel, it is written, "offered a more excellent sacrifice than Cain." We are led to ask, What made it more excellent? The superiority is not in the fact that he first of all offered a sacrifice of blood or even the best of the flock, but rather that it was in faith. God considered it acceptable and of eternal worth, blessing him with a heavenly reward. In His own way God conveyed to Abel that he was righteous. Romans tells us "that there is none righteous, no, not one" (Rom. 3:10). We further know that no man can become righteous without the shedding of blood. Because Abel, a sinful person, came in faith with an offering that involved the shedding of blood, his sacrifice pointed to the sacrifice of the Old Testament system. All of this system pointed to the sacrifice of Jesus Christ, and Abel showed — even though dimly — that he believed in Christ as the atonement for sin. Therefore, he was declared righteous.

There is another point to notice. Cain was a "good" man. Genesis says that it was he who took the initiative in bringing an offering. Cain came first and Abel followed. Again, Cain also brought an offering to the true God. He, too, must have realized that his sins demanded some type of satisfaction, some atonement. He was theologically sound, no doubt, because he realized that he was not righteous before God, but a sinner. In his offering, the sin does not seem to be that he brought the first fruits of the ground, for this type of offering was also permissible later on under Old Testament ritual. In fact it could have complemented the offering of Abel's blood gift. His sin consisted rather in one or two faults: he did not also bring a bloody sacrifice and he did not offer in faith. Apparently, his heart was not in the offering. He appeared to take the first thing that came to his attention and offered that. His "goodness" was that of a work-righteous offering without a true faith, that is, faith in the promise of Genesis 3:15, which is basically faith in the coming Messiah. He did not possess, therefore, the right kind of Old Testament faith in the coming Messiah who was to shed His blood as an offering for sin. Cain's offering was a self-righteous sacrifice, a work-righteous gift. Because his heart was not right, as seen in God's rejection of his sacrifice, jealousy, anger, and hatred against God and against his brother Abel led him to murder his brother. Abel died a martyr to the faith.

The second hero of faith is Enoch. It is interesting to note how differently God dealt with these heroes. Abel believed and lost his life through murder. Enoch believed and did not die, but was translated by God from earth to heaven without passing through the valley of the shadow of death. Enoch also had witness borne to him that he was righteous. That is the common testimony God gives to those who believe in the atoning work of Jesus Christ. Why God should have dealt with Enoch as He did, we do not know. Was his faith that much stronger and richer? Did he, by faith, live in such close fellowship with God that in a sense the two, walking together, agreed so closely that hopeful of Christ's coming, even though dimly, "the same mind being in him as it was in Christ Jesus," God unexpectedly took him home with Him into heaven? Certainly he "pleased" God; for verse 6 tells us that "without faith it is impossible to please him," which indicates that Enoch indeed did please God.

In this contrast between Abel and Enoch we see that even the degree of faith that we possess is the gift of God. Or look at it another way. Even if the faith of Abel and Enoch were of the same degree of quality and quantity, God deals with each one according as He sees fit. Further, in contrasting Abel and Enoch, the lesson that God wants taught may be that each believer must be content with God's individual dealings with him. Also, whether we live or die, we live and die by faith. This the author wanted the Hebrews to understand: if they had to suffer they should suffer in faith; if they had an easier life it had to be lived by faith.

The next person considered in this catalog of faithful witnesses is Noah. Does divine revelation wish to bring out a progress, a lesson, in the development of faith uniquely in these heroes? Are all these people a tremendous, overwhelming example of the same thing; or does each one of them illustrate a specific added detail to the overall teaching? Naturally all of them together demonstrate one grand lesson, that God's grace in their lives made them have faith and because of that faith they all were more than conquerors. But each one has his own contribution to make. Just as Abel's faith made him offer a bloody sacrifice, which indicated at that early stage that he knew he could be righteous only by faith in the shedding of Christ's blood, and Enoch's faith led him to live intimately and trustingly with God, so Noah's faith in Christ in whom alone is salvation made him work for the preserving of his household. Humanly speaking, this faith of Noah, leading to his being spared in the flood, made possible the coming of Christ; for if everyone had been destroyed at the time of the flood, Christ would not have come.

Noah's faith is also an indication that once a man has faith he will go on working in spite of the ridicule of men and long delay on the part of God in carrying out His plan. After all, Noah worked 120 years before the flood came. All through those years of waiting Noah was also witnessing, for we read that he was "a preacher of righteousness" (II Peter 2:5). That would make his life much harder. He preached and showed by the building of the ark that he expected the judgment of God. The scoffers must have given him a rough time when year after year no flood came. In spite of it he continued preaching because he believed God was true and would eventually do what He had said.

These three examples — Abel, Enoch, and Noah — make up the witness of faith in the period before the flood. In that day of wickedness God had His faithful witnesses. God has His witnesses today also, and we should determine if each of us is one.

These three men of faith are presented here to illustrate three aspects of God's dealings in the Old Testament promises that foreshadowed the coming of Christ and the carrying out of God's promises and warnings. Abel points ahead from that early history to the fact that without the shedding of blood there is no remission of sin. Somehow he was led to believe this. Enoch proves that by faith, when blood has been shed, fellowship with God is personal, constant, and real; for he walked with God. The record of Noah illustrates that if one does not believe in God and walk with Him in faith, judgment is certain to come. Noah patiently preached this, all the while believing in God, so that he and his family were spared from destruction.

Lesson 13

Questions, Topics, Suggestions for further study

1. Why had the author of chapter 10 referred to Habakkuk 2:3 ff., and particularly the latter part of verse 4? How does that quotation serve as a fit introduction to chapter 11?

2. What has chapter 11 frequently been called and why?

3. If the chapter does not open with a theological definition of faith, what is the author trying to convey?

4. What purpose does the writer have in presenting all these heroes of faith?

5. Describe why Abel's sacrifice was better than Cain's.

6. State why Cain may be called a "good" man, while actually he was
a bad man. How did Cain prove his badness?

7. What are the distinguishing marks of Abel, Enoch, and Noah?

8. How did Noah bear his testimony?

9. Make a list of at least five of the heroes of faith and describe what
marks they had that we should possess today.

a.

b.

c.

d.

e.

10. Define the term "patriarch" and write a description of one.

11. Trace through other books of the Bible and list at least three passages that have something to say on faith.

a.

b.

c.

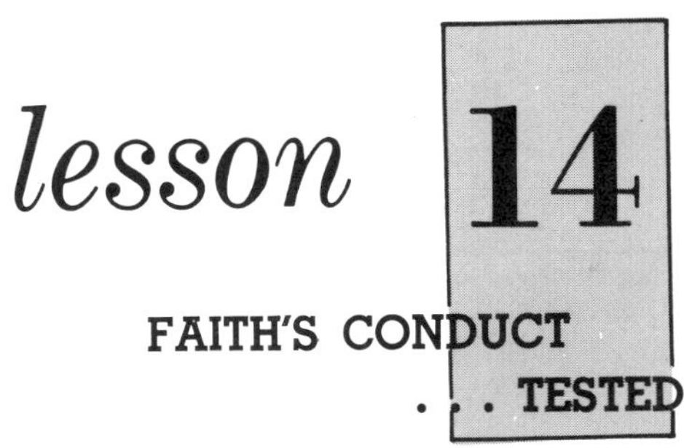

lesson 14

FAITH'S CONDUCT
. . . TESTED

Hebrews 11 (II)

The second section of chapter 11, from verses 17-40, deals with three aspects of faith: the activity of faith, the power of faith, and the endurance of faith. The writer demonstrates these aspects of faith in the lives of all the Old Testament saints, beginning in this section with Abraham, the father of the covenant of grace, and going on through the suffering, martyred heroes of faith of all the ages. All these saints had three marks in common: (1) they all had spiritual and moral weaknesses; (2) they experienced persecutions in their lives; and (3) they had an enduring faith in God. In spite of their weaknesses or the afflictions that others heaped on them, they "had witness borne to them through their faith" that God had better things in store for them — peace, glory, and eternal life in God's presence in heaven. This they obtained completely when they died, remaining true to the faith through His grace.

This section begins the listing of the heroes of faith with Abraham and includes Jacob, the father of the twelve tribes and the father of Israel, the people and nation of God. But the section carries us beyond the nation of Israel and introduces us to the Gentile involvement in faith. It shows Jacob blessing a mixed people, the sons of Joseph, as well as telling of Joseph who became to all external purposes, through God's specific leading, a Gentile himself — even marrying a Gentile woman. This section also shows the people of God in their Gentile surroundings and dealings: Joseph, who was a captive and slave in Egypt and yet by faith triumphed and became a ruler there; Moses, who grew up in Egypt and took the children of Israel out of the land. He was reared in riches, banished to poverty, and yet triumphed through faith to become Israel's deliverer and messiah. Even the Gentile Rahab is mentioned, she who was a pagan innkeeper of ill reputation, whom the children of Israel met as they came into the promised land.

The point is that faith is universally essential and is triumphant, making all these heroes — sinful and weak though they were — victorious. The further point is that faith is not the inheritance of one national or socially and economically accepted group. It is a gift of God, and when possessed by His children it is active (living) and has power to overcome difficulties and to endure.

To return to the first of the patriarchs, Abraham, as the father of the faithful, literally lived from start to finish by faith. The passage opens with a demonstration of Abraham's faith for, when he received God's call to leave his homeland of Ur in the Chaldees, he obeyed God implicitly. One characteristic of Abraham's faith was his obedience, even though there are several unpleasant things about his life at this juncture. First of all it appears that the company took their gods with them; hence they were idolatrous. Second, he did delay for a time in Haran instead of going directly to the promised land. In spite of those difficulties that showed him to be a man of like sinful nature and character as all the rest, the book of Hebrews does not touch on them but demonstrates that he was a man of enduring faith, obedient to God's commands. God is not ashamed of Abraham, the reason being that already in his day Abraham's sins were forgiven through the Christ. When God looked on Abraham, He saw His beloved Son's robe of righteousness surrounding him, and therefore accepted Abraham through faith, even though he needed refining and disciplining to build up that faith. God therefore said, "I am not ashamed to acknowledge this man as one of My children."

Verse 6 states that all these heroes had faith; therefore "they were well pleasing to God" in spite of their shortcomings and faults. Abraham also is the first hero of faith mentioned after the flood. After the flood it seemed men did not lead the separate life and so God, instead of adopting a people that was worldly, separated to Himself a people of His own choice to make of them a separated spiritual people. He begins that work of separation with Abraham, who obeyed the call. But God still was interested also in the world; for He promised to bless Abraham and his seed, and through Abraham the blessings were also promised to the world. The Lord Jesus Christ, the Savior of the world, was the great promise for the world.

Abraham's wife too is singled out as a heroine of faith. The testimony about Sarah from verse 11 is that in spite of her unbelief (as brought out by the word "even") she too, by faith, gave birth to a son when she was past age. This son, in turn, became the father of an innumerable multitude. Sarah had given up hope of having a child years before, and when the announcement came to her that she would bear a son she laughed in unbelief. Somewhere along the line, faith was awakened in her, most likely sometime after the heavenly message came to Abraham. She came to believe the heavenly promise with the result that she is recorded as one of the heroines of faith.

In the commentary on Abraham, these acts or virtues are singled out as distinguishing marks of his faith:
1. By faith Abraham *obeyed* God (vs. 8).
2. By faith Abraham *became* a sojourner in the land (vs. 9).
3. By faith Abraham *looked* for the heavenly city (vs. 10).
4. By faith Abraham *believed* the promise of God (vss. 13-16, 17).
5. By faith Abraham *offered* Isaac (vss. 17-19).

Verse 13, with one sweep swinging back to Abel, Enoch, through Noah, then on to Abraham and Sarah, states, "These all died in faith." Verse 39 reads, "These all . . . received not the promise." These therefore all died with the promise in their hearts, but did not see the promise fulfilled. The fact is they died in the *way* of faith, holding fast to it. Though they did not see the promise realized, they believed to their last breath that it was true. That essentially is the way of true religion. This expression applies also to Enoch who did not die. Enoch's being taken by God is pictured as having died, even as the rest. In other words, death is a taking of the saint from one realm to another; and whether it be by means of going through the grave or being snatched into the air, the method is not the most important thing.

With verse 17 we have the trial or testing of Abraham's faith in the offering of Isaac. Scripture tells us that Abraham obeyed God, "accounting that God is able to raise him up, even from the dead; from whence he did also in a figure receive him back." Abraham went up Mount Moriah with a faith that knew he would come back with his son, thinking that after literally offering him God would raise Isaac from the dead. Proof of this is seen in the fact that Abraham ordered his servants to remain behind at the foot of the mountain, stating, "Abide ye here with the ass, and I and the lad will go yonder, and we will worship, and *come again unto you*" (Gen. 22:5). In talking to Isaac after he asked his father about the lamb, Abraham said, "God will provide himself the lamb for a burnt-offering." God did just that.

In the cases of Isaac, Jacob, and Joseph, the episodes recorded are taken from deathbed scenes. These men not only lived by faith, but in the hour of death their faith made them look beyond the immediate present to the vast future when faith would be made sight. In dying these men trusted God, believing His promises. In triumphant faith they spoke their blessings to and exacted promises from those who would succeed them.

The next section, which is the major section of the chapter, is devoted to Abraham and Moses. Abraham was the father of the covenant people; Moses was the father of the law, the rule of conduct for the covenant people. Here in Hebrews the life or the faith of Moses starts out with the faith of his parents. Faith is first of all a gift of God, implanted by Him and continued from father to son through many generations, always through personal commitments somewhere in the lives of those involved. It is never a matter of inheritance but of earnest prayer and training and humble acceptance.

Here are the events singled out in the life of Moses as compared with Abraham's life:
1. By faith Moses *was hidden* for three months (vs. 23).
2. By faith Moses *refused* to be called a son of Pharaoh's daughter (vs. 24).
3. By faith Moses *chose* to suffer ill treatment with God's people (vs. 25).
4. By faith Moses *forsook* Egypt (vs. 27).
5. By faith Moses *kept* the Passover (vs. 28).

These characteristic actions of Moses seem different from those of Abraham. Moses' faith is marked by action carried out under testings and trials. The normal aspect of faith seems to be that it flourishes and grows strong under such conditions. The normal Christian life, in fact, as learned from the Bible and church history, in its very nature includes testing, trials, and often severe persecution.

How far did this faith of the Old Testament heroes center in the conscious recognition and understanding that Jesus Christ was the coming Messiah? The text reads concerning Moses that he "accounted the reproach of Christ greater riches than the treasures of Egypt." A note in the margin of the American Revised Version is that the expression "of Christ" can be "of *the* Christ," which makes it clear that Moses anticipated the Lord Jesus Christ. Moses bore his shame and reproach as a type of Christ and, in his own consciousness, for the sake of Christ. Shame, persecution, trial, and temptation need to be borne and understood in the light of Christ and His suffering. As a result these trials are actually faith endured because of "the foolishness of the cross." In the Old Testament the heroes bore this by a faith that anticipated Christ's coming; in the New Testament this is endured as witness and proof of the reality and power of faith through Christ's accomplished work.

During the time of Moses, great things happened: the giving of the law, the celebration of the passover, the exodus from Egypt, and the life of the people in the bondage of the desert. Through all this time Moses as God's appointed leader lived not by sight first of all, but by faith. Faith is the key word to all this history. Only when the people lacked faith did they get into trouble. The miracles which occurred in that day were interwoven with faith, even though it was often weak. The people of Israel — above all Moses as their head — had to live by faith. When Moses' faith failed and he became angry and smote the rock instead of speaking to it, God forbade him to enter the promised land. God wanted the people to know that they were different from the surrounding nations. They had to live by implicit faith in Him. When faith was lacking on the part of their leader, Moses, God could not pass it by but had to show His displeasure.

As with Abraham, the writer does not enlarge on Moses' weaknesses, although Moses did show some fear. Instead, it is stated that Moses, even though the Bible says he did not fear the "wrath of the king," fled from Pharaoh. He did not wish to enter Pharaoh's presence because he was afraid. When he exercised faith, and only then, Moses became strong and dared to face the wrath of the king. It was faith, finally, that kept the angel of death out of the midst of the camp of Israel for we read, "By faith he kept the passover, and the sprinkling of the blood, that the destroyer of the first-born should not touch them" (vs. 28). The overall picture of the life of Moses was one of strong faith and full commitment to God.

Verses 30 and 31 indicate that Joshua, under whose leadership the walls of Jericho fell, is not mentioned while Rahab is. In these two verses there are two aspects of faith. The first is that when weak, frail human beings have faith, wonders and miracles happen. How utterly impossible was the situation of these weak, milling multitudes conquering the walls of Jericho. But God's power provided the added dynamo of faith necessary to conquer. Instead of attacking the walls, they marched around them until miraculously and victoriously the walls caved in without use of arms and might. The second picture is that of a harlot, who, even though she was a Gentile and a bad woman, was saved by faith. She believed God and it was counted to her for righteousness.

When the writer has sufficiently proved that the patriarchs and early leaders, far removed in time from Christ, truly manifested an active, powerful, and enduring faith, he stops the enumeration of names with the time of the judges. He changes from concentration on individuals and instead now groups these heroes under the accomplishments that their faith rendered. From verses 32-40 he shows what faith accomplished through these heroes. Some are mentioned and others are left unmentioned, perhaps because everyone knew who they were — Daniel, Isaiah, and Jeremiah, for example. In this section, therefore, the writer —

1. Tells about what faith accomplished through these heroes.
2. Shows what obstacles and trials the faithful had to overcome.
3. Shows that their faith kept them true to the end even though they did not realize or obtain in actuality that which they believed was true. The reason was that "apart from us they should not be made perfect."

The names do not appear in chronological order; in fact, Samuel is the last one named. It is not that one is more important than another, but rather that Samuel, for instance, belongs with the prophets who are mentioned as a group but not by name. It is not the time of history that counts, but it is the fact of faith in every age that is significant.

As one reads the names of these heroes, he could try to fit the deed that is spoken about — such as "subduing kingdoms" and "stopping the mouths of lions" — with the name of a prophet or king who is unnamed, as the one to whom this event might apply. For instance, one could think of Daniel, the prophet, as the one who stopped the mouths of lions. Probably the writer did not have any one specific person in mind for each specific event related, but he was thinking of several who accomplished great deeds of faith. He is looking over the whole field of Old Testament heroes, and all of them together accomplished all these noble deeds by the triumph of faith. In this way he lets his reader think of whatever person he wishes as the example.

For study purposes, then, try fitting the various characters of history with the deeds that are here listed. For instance, when it comes to subduing kingdoms, these might qualify: David, who was the great master at military victory, or Joshua, who gained the victories in the promised land. When it comes to stopping the mouths of lions one thinks of these: Samson (Judg. 14:6), David (I Sam. 17:34), and Daniel (Dan. 6:16). One could go through all the Old Testament history and fit names to the events related. Some even lost their lives, for tradition tells us that Jeremiah died by the sword and Isaiah "was sawn asunder."

As the chapter closes, it is well to recall how it began. Verse 2 reads: "The elders had witness borne to them." All these heroes, named and unnamed, had witness borne to them that their faith was genuine and would eventually be vindicated. Yet, as we come to the end of the chapter, although they had witness borne to them, they did not receive the fulfillment of the promise. So faith seems to be foolishness, for what did it profit them? They did not obtain what they looked forward to obtaining, after all. To the contrary, faith will bring them the reward, the same reward our faith will bring us: "the salvation of the Messiah in a better country." These saints by faith went to heaven where their souls were safely kept in anticipation of the coming Messiah. When He came and gained the victory, their faith gained for them the thing they believed in — triumph through Jesus Christ forever — joyous life in His presence.

The point of the closing words of the chapter is that all believers of all ages, of both Testaments, will be made perfect, or complete, at the same time. Even though the saints who have gone on before have already successfully completed the journey and their struggle is over, the fact that they reached their goal before us makes no difference in respect to full and complete victory. When Jesus Christ returns in the fullness of His glory, we shall all at that time finally be made perfect and complete. Then we shall all receive the realization of that which we and they had believed. We, together with them at the same moment, will obtain the full blessing. At that point faith will be vindicated and all will experience the victory of faith becoming sight.

In the closing verses (32-40) there is a view of history that merits consideration. The writer looks on God's plan for His people of all ages as essentially one. Many forget that fact when they divide history into compartments or dispensations. God is saying here that actually there is only one dispensation in all of human history — the dispensation of grace — and the essential element for men in that dispensation is faith. The faith which the Old Testament saint had is exactly the same qualitatively as that which the New Testament person confesses, as well as that which the believer has today. When the full perfection is reached we shall all receive the glorious full revelation of the Lord Jesus Christ at the same time. Today, when faith seems to be waning and when testings are increasing, this is a wonderful assurance. To be a Christian is a glorious thing and we should rejoice in the fact that we are so privileged. This should give us an incentive to better living through Christ. This should lead us to strive for a strong and virile faith.

Lesson 14

Questions, Topics, Suggestions for further study

1. Give your view as to why women are mentioned in this group of heroes of faith.

2. List the points that are singled out in Abraham's life and presented in this chapter.

3. Give a paragraph on Abraham's faith, which made him believe he would keep or get back Isaac even though he offered him to God.

4. Why do we have the deathbed scenes of Isaac, Jacob, and Joseph before us?

5. What events are recorded here from Moses' life? How do they compare to those recorded of Abraham?

6. What happened to Moses when he lacked faith, and what did God want to show by forbidding Moses to enter the promised land?

7. What three things are offered to the reader in verses 32-40?

   a.

   b.

   c.

8. When is our faith and that of the Old Testament saints made perfect?

9. What view of history does chapter 11 present?

10. State what chapter 11 means to you and one or two points you learned about it in your present study.

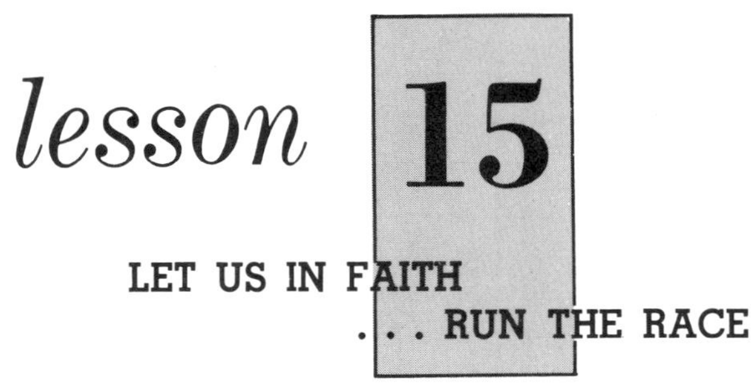

lesson 15

LET US IN FAITH
. . . RUN THE RACE

Hebrews 12

I. Run patiently, surrounded by witnesses and looking to Jesus (vss. 1-13).

II. Follow peace and sanctification and God will be seen (vss. 14-17).

III. Refuse not Him that speaketh and grace will be sure (vss. 18-29).

All these centuries of faithful heroes add up to a strong testimony of faith's worth. In the light of these heroes of faith of chapter 11 and their victorious life, we are exhorted to continue steadfast in the Christian journey. The word used for journey is "contest" or "race," while in the book of Acts we are reminded of the "way." Here it is the contest or struggle in that way.

In this race we are to lay aside every weight. Those weights are not in themselves sinful, but are matters that hold us back from putting forth our utmost. A weight is unnecessary baggage, that which we would ordinarily strip away as a hindrance in the race. It hinders our speed and keeps us from gaining the victory. In the case of an athlete it refers to too much clothing or too much flesh or obesity which he would have to eliminate before being able to achieve. There is a difference between "weight" and "sin"; yet it is stated that both must be put aside and "weight" is stated first.

For the Christian there can be no halfway measures. He must get rid of sin, but he certainly needs to eliminate excess baggage also. The kind of sin described here may be a favorite pet sin. Generally, it is thought of in terms of sin that clings to us like a close fitting, binding garment, impeding every step of our progress. It is easier to get enmeshed and enwrapped with sin than to break with it, and as a result this directive is given. All our effort and full commitment are demanded. We can never be satisfied with an avoidance of sin only; we need the added effort of doing away with the nonessentials and be wholly ready and equipped for the struggle.

The "so great a cloud of witnesses" refers to all the heroes in the previous chapter. In this case the term "witness" does not necessarily emphasize the martyr angle, although in chapter 11 martyrs are included; but it means testimony to what they themselves have experienced. The witnesses, having experienced the deeds and trials recorded, were encouraging those still in the race.

To what actually were they witnessing? Some contend they were testifying to the fact that if one continues to run the race, stays in the race, and keeps on running, that is, endures, he will obtain the reward. These heroes seem to be saying, "We did — so keep courage." That, indirectly, may be true, but it is not the essential message. Deep down they are saying, "We are witnessing to the grace of God. We were sinners of like passions with you; we were subjected to the same temptations you battle, but by the grace of God we finally conquered. We are witnessing to you that the grace of God will see you through so that you, like us, will gain the victory. For that reason, you should not just sit back, but you should lay aside every weight and sin and run, but run with patience, not becoming discouraged and not stopping along the way thinking that you will never make it anyhow. True, in your own strength you would not; but because of God's grace you certainly will."

Although we are compassed about by so great a cloud of witnesses, these witnesses do not so completely surround us that they obscure our vision of Jesus Christ. We are not first of all to look at the heroes of faith but only look to them as they witness of God's grace to them. We are constantly to keep our eyes on Jesus. When we look to Him, several things are seen that are of interest:

1. He is originator (author) and completer (finisher) of faith. In other words, there would be no faith in us nor would it continue if it were not for Christ. We therefore must stay true to Him.
2. Christ saw a joyful end to His work. We ought to consider our end in that joyful light, particularly in view of the fact that Christ has already opened the way for us. In looking to Jesus there would be a bright gleam shining through the afflictions these Hebrews endured.
3. He endured the cross and despised the shame.
4. He sat down at the right hand of God after He had gained the victory, proving thereby that He was victorious. As we look at that Christ, we gain a vision of our own victory, by His grace surmounting all trials that are certain to come.

Chapter 12 opens with Jesus victorious and now sitting at the right hand of God. That fact ought to be of encouragement to those who are being tested for their faith, encouraging them in the light of the victories of the Old Testament heroes of faith in chapter 11 and Christ's victory in chapter 12. In chapter 12 the writer is exhorting his readers to stay with it because they were becoming discouraged and some seemed ready to quit the Christian race. He tells them that it isn't as bad as they think, for not one had yet resisted to the point of the shedding of blood. He admonishes them to consider what Jesus endured for them and to see Him as One who took on Himself the form of a servant, succeeded in living in their world, suffering more than they would ever have to suffer. Thinking on that magnificent sacrifice, they should not wax weary or faint.

The writer also wants his readers to realize that they should be prepared for chastening, just as it had been experienced in the Old Testament. They must remember that it is an indication of the love of God toward those whom He chastens. In fact, chastening is a normal experience in the Christian life.

When the hearers compare their sufferings with those of the Lord Jesus, they will see how much greater His were than theirs; hence they ought to be able to bear theirs graciously and patiently. They will realize that in His love God is chastening them as preparation for their eternal reward as He did His Son Jesus Christ, who is now exalted at the throne on the right hand of the Father. Even though we do not understand the reason for the Lord's loving chastening in our lives, the fact remains that it comes to us in His wisdom and overruling love. He who constantly avoids chastening may well question whether he is a legitimate son of God. These things are hard to comprehend, but natural fathers discipline their children for their best interest. Christians therefore should not be alarmed when their heavenly Father causes His children to be tested.

Although this disciplining is by no means pleasant while one experiences it, after it is all over it produces a blessed fruit. In view of all that, the readers are exhorted to take courage. The application to Hebrews 12:1-11 is found in Hebrews 12:12, 13.

The addressees of this letter give a picture of almost defeat and despair, for they are called to lift up their hanging hands and strengthen their shuffling, weakened feet. There may be in those words a return to the first two verses of the chapter, which deal with the Christian race. More likely, however, the picture is one of general weakness, with the writer trying to challenge these Christians to perk up so they will be living the fuller Christian life. Even the road on which they were walking seemed to be crooked and they are exhorted to straighten that path. Maybe they were wobbling about and are therefore instructed to walk a straight path. This is an exhortation to the individual as a believer, but also to the community at large, to share and help with each other's burdens. Those who have been experiencing the disciplining of God and have been strengthened by it ought to be the ones to help the weak and unstable strugglers. As one writer puts it, "Whether their state grew worse or better depended on the care exercised in the removal of the stumbling blocks" (*The Century Bible*, Vol. 16, p. 229).

What is the unevenness that the writer is concerned about in this letter? Most likely it is the hesitation these people showed in choosing between Judaism with its legalism and Christianity with its true freedom. The writer may have been referring to wrong practices that followed in their lives because they did not remain strong in fighting off temptation. If the whole Christian fellowship followed a straight path, it would be much easier for the weak to walk along in that Christian way. Pursuing a "plain path" would lead to a better life for all who were in the Christian community.

The first section ends with verse 13. It ends — as so many passages do in this book — with a hopeful thought. There is healing if only they will pursue the right way. Christianity is a hopeful, helpful religion. It, and it alone, gives healing to the infirm and weak, restoration to the sinner, and above all joy to its adherents.

The second section, which begins with verse 14, is an exhortation to pursue and fight for peace. In this world one can never expect to sit back, confusing a sense of peace with inertia and a state of doing nothing. Peace comes only after war, so the Christian must constantly be fighting against evil not only as it is "out there," but especially in his own life and the lives of those around him. In the light of what follows, this peace the readers are to pursue is not a doctrinal matter in the sense that they are to see to it that everyone is pure in doctrine (that, of course, is also exceedingly necessary); but the emphasis is on a peace in connection with purity of life. It is the peace of a pure life, including sanctification, which means that one will endeavor to live in harmony with his neighbors and will not be quarreling and deceiving and living wrongly. This peace is possible only through sanctification. The writer is specific. Such sanctification is obtained only through the blood of our Lord Jesus Christ. As the Gospel of Matthew also states, a man cannot see God unless he is pure in heart (Matt. 5:8).

The author had spoken of this subject previously when he wrote of having a "cleansed conscience." The thought is that everyone should see that the membership of the body of Christ is kept at such a high level of spiritual life that no one will go wrong and quarrel or backslide. To this end, all are to exercise oversight, the one over the other. These verses direct us to the right attitude and conduct toward men: "follow peace with all men"; "sanctification toward him."

Next follows the conclusion. When men do not seek after peace and sanctification, certain dangers attend them and serious evil consequences can result. The readers are to guard against at least four possible evils:
1. Lest there should be any man who falls short of the grace of God (vs. 15).
2. Lest any root of bitterness springing up trouble them (vs. 15).
3. Lest there should be any fornicator (vs. 16).
4. Lest there should be any profane person (vs. 16).

To drive home the lesson to the readers (the Christian community), the writer uses the illustration of that profane person Esau, whose "god was his belly" and who lived for the gratification of the flesh to such an extent that he made mockery of the covenant by selling his birthright for a mess of pottage (cf. Gen. 27). Later Esau sorrowed because he did not obtain the birthright blessing from his father.

There are two interpretations possible for the expression "For he found no place for a change of mind in his father, though he sought it diligently with tears" (vs. 17). The first is that Esau sought repentance with tears, but the deed stood and could not be changed; hence no remedy was possible. He may not have been genuine in his tears, not having true sorrow for sin. One rather hesitates to say that if a man truly seeks repentance he cannot find it. Such seems to militate against the teachings of Scripture. Therefore, Esau did not *truly* seek it. The second explanation is that he tried with deepest tears of anguish to change his father's mind regarding the birthright, but that was impossible for Isaac had spoken under divine inspiration and he was powerless to change what had been said. The latter of the two thoughts seems preferable.

The third and last section of the chapter comprises verses 18-29. The reader is earnestly warned to listen to and heed the voice of God. This is the last warning of the entire book, and the writer wishes to make it as impressive as possible.

C. Erdman has this to say on the passage under consideration: "In this paragraph the argument of the epistle reaches its climax. The first parenthetic, but essential warning was against neglect, 2:1-4; the second was against unbelief, 3:7—4:14; the third against falling away, 5:11—6:20; the fourth against willful sin, 10:26-31. Here the warning is summarized in a single sentence: 'See that ye refuse not him that speaketh.' All five are designed to carry out the supreme purpose of the epistle, which is to secure loyalty to Christ and to prevent the readers from turning away from him" (*The Epistle to the Hebrews*, p. 128).

The reference to Esau in the Old Testament and the fact of his living according to the flesh bring to mind the condemnation brought out in the Old Testament against those who lived by law instead of grace. That is a guide to the New Testament and its message of grace. It is Sinai and Zion contrasted, for the New Testament readers ought to live by Zion. But if they want to live by Sinai, their judgment will be worse than that of Esau. We are reminded of the contrasts in chapter 10 where the two dispensations were introduced. The former was visible, the latter invisible; the former in a sense carnal, the latter spiritual; the former of the earth, the latter from heaven.

The thought the writer wishes to bring out in connection with Sinai and Zion is that these readers had actually come to Mount Zion. It was not a future event. That is true of every person who professes faith in the Lord Jesus Christ. It is impossible then for the dedicated Christian to live a profane life. These Hebrew Christians had come, in contrast to the Judaism of former days:

1. To Mount Zion (vs. 22).
2. To the city of the living God, the new, heavenly Jerusalem (vs. 22).
3. To myriads of angels, the innumerable heavenly hosts (vs. 22).
4. To the assembly of the firstborn who are enrolled in heaven — this is the invisible, the true church of Jesus Christ (vs. 23).
5. To God, the judge of all men (vs. 23).
6. To the spirits of just men made perfect (vs. 23).
7. To Jesus, the mediator of the new covenant (vs. 24).
8. To the blood of sprinkling (that is, the blood of Christ) that speaketh better than that of Abel (vs. 24).

Their faith had led them to all this when they professed to believe in the Lord Jesus Christ as their Savior. They had walked in this reality and confession by faith and not by sight. They would much rather, as to their carnal and earthly nature, see the things to which they had come

— such as Mount Sinai, a law written on tables of stone, God appearing in smoke and fire and thunderings. Their faith, however, is far higher and better; and having come to all these wonderful things, they should beware and listen to the voice of God, seeing with spiritual eyes and not backsliding.

It is commonly accepted by Bible students that Israel would remember three mountains. The first one was Mount Moriah, where God tested Abraham and gave him back his son Isaac, making the birth of Christ possible. The second was Mount Sinai, where God gave the law. The third was Mount Zion, where the temple and spiritual worship were. Mount Zion, or Mount Sion, is the high place of grace. It is the new Jerusalem, the city of the living God. Calvin called this the church. That mountain was visible, but it had to be seen by faith and by the eye of faith alone.

Although there was trembling on Mount Moriah when Abraham lifted his knife to slay Isaac — even though he had faith to believe that God would raise his son from the dead, and although there were quakings and trembling on Mount Sinai with the manifestations of God's power and majesty at the giving of the law, on Mount Zion there was no trembling for there faith triumphed and stood unshaken. These were the things that could not be shaken: the voice of God, the promises, God's wrath, God's love, and the church. That voice of God must be heeded, for His Word is eternal. God will keep His promises. God's church or kingdom will abide forever. God's love is eternal, and even His wrath and His threats will stand also!

For that reason the writer is so solemn in his warning. What an awful and majestic way to end the chapter — on a note of terrible warning! "For our God is a consuming fire." But we may approach our God with love, for He gave His Son for us. Yet we must approach Him with awe and reverence, for even in His love we need to remember that He is a consuming fire. How thankful we may be that He loved us and gave His Son for us! Because we walk by faith in His grace, the majesty of His judgment will never punish us. In that confidence we love and serve Him — not under law, but with the law helping us to serve Him in grace and faith.

Lesson 15
Questions, Topics, Suggestions for further study

1. What is the Christian exhorted to do as chapter 12 opens? How is the race or journey described?

2. What is the difference between "weight" and "sin"? Why must both be discarded?

3. Define the term "witness" as used in this chapter.

4. What is the witness that those triumphant heroes impress on us?

5. What do we see when we look to Jesus?

6. What are the reasons for the exhortations in verses 12 and 13?

7. As the second section of the chapter begins, the reader is exhorted to "battle" after peace. Why is this expressed as a battle?

8. What relationship are we to sustain to our fellowmen and what relationship are we to hold toward God?

9. If men do not seek after peace and sanctification, what four dangers beset them?

a.   c.

b.   d.

10. What purpose does the history of Esau serve in this chapter?

11. What solemn warning is found in the last section of the chapter?

12. List again the warning sections of the book of Hebrews.

13. To what have the New Testament Christians come?

14. What are the meanings of the three mountains?

15. What is the reason for ending the chapter with the statement, "For our God is a consuming fire"? How may a Christian take comfort from that expression?

lesson 16

THE ETERNAL CHRIST . . . GIVER OF PEACE

Hebrews 13

I. Exhortations to love the brothers and strangers (vss. 1-6)

II. Advice on Christian practices (vss. 7-12)

III. Invitation to go to Jesus Christ outside the camp (vss. 13-19)

IV. Concluding benediction (vss. 20-25)

Chapter 13 continues the practical exhortations begun in chapter 12. The first injunctions deal with our personal or individual life; the next series deals with our religious or doctrinal duties, including an injunction regarding our attitude toward those in spiritual and ecclesiastical authority.

As in other chapters, there are at least two texts that stand out as highlights and should be memorized:

1. "Jesus Christ is the same yesterday and today, yea, and forever" (13:8).
2. "Now the God of peace, who brought again from the dead the great shepherd of the sheep with the blood of an eternal covenant, even our Lord Jesus, make you perfect in every good thing to do his will, working in us that which is well-pleasing in his sight, through Jesus Christ: to whom be the glory forever and ever. Amen" (13:20, 21).

The chapter opens with a twofold exhortation to love the brothers and strangers. Quite naturally the immediate household of faith comes first, but almost in the same breath comes the injunction to love strangers. On that latter count a mission method is obvious. One of the ways to interest strangers in the gospel of the Lord Jesus Christ is to show them love. Love speaks louder than many sermons and helps win the distant ones to the Lord. Of course strangers need to hear the gospel, but while doing so, they must be shown love.

The seriousness and intense emotion under which the book was written is seen in the threefold command for the readers to take all these thoughts to heart and apply them to everyday Christian life. So important is the need of staying true to the gospel that the writer three times — once negatively and twice positively — ordered his readers to remember constantly these truths:

"Forget not to show love unto strangers" (13:2).
"Remember them that are in bonds" (13:3).
"Remember them that had the rule over you" (13:7).

The areas covered are in the realm of practical Christian living. This is seen in their conduct toward strangers who might come into the focus of these Christians and, not having a home, would be in danger of being swallowed up by the world. If these strangers were not Christians, to show them love by taking them into their homes would be an excellent way of witnessing to the love of God and Christ. This in turn might well open the door to the preaching of the gospel and even salvation.

The second group are the destitute ones in prison and the ill treated. These suffering ones would need help, and their lot was a possible prediction of what might happen to the Christians for standing true to the faith. In sharing their love and help with these tested ones, God could be strengthening their faith for future trials. This action would also serve to get their minds off their own lesser trials.

All this would lead to a strengthening of faith because the truth of the statement: "The Lord is my helper; I will not fear: What shall man do unto me?" (13:6) would come from their hearts as a confession of their experience and confidence in God.

The position of leadership in the church and the abilities of "them that had the rule" over the other Christians would stand out as an example of Christian strength and endurance as the leaders face opposition. The readers are commanded to "imitate their faith." And if they would prove true now, right now, they had guarantee that this was proof of their faithfulness in the gospel for tomorrow, because "Jesus Christ is the same yesterday, and today, yea and forever" (13:8). Once truly redeemed, they were forever secure; but they had to work at remaining true, lest they prove they were not actually redeemed.

The reference to angels may go back to the time Abraham and Lot encountered these angels and entertained them. By entertaining strangers we may be receiving angels in disguise, and by not entertaining them we would be disobeying the Word of the Lord. The joyful word in the day of judgment from Christ is, "I was a stranger and ye took me in." Is your home a guest house for strangers for the Lord's sake?

The less blessed, the prisoners of affliction, are to be remembered. To remember is to bring to focus some latent thought which may have been lodged in the mind as a former instruction, command, or happening with the purpose of showing some action.

The readers are next called on to be pure in thought and conduct, guarding well the sanctity of family life. In these days of high divorce rate and lax moral and sexual living, it is good to listen again to the ancient inspired words: "fornicators and adulterers God will judge" (13:4). It is difficult for the Christian to remain pure in thought and deed when the world is bombarding him with suggestive and immoral literature and propaganda. This may well be the trial of our faith in our day — and we should be strong in our fight against this as well as other forms of evil. Chastity, purity, and love are virtues to be diligently cultivated.

These readers are also to be free from the love of money, knowing that God takes care of His children even though at times they may have only a crust of bread. The individuals are warned about allowing the external and material aspects of life to play too prominent a role. These same injunctions are sound in this day of affluence and laxity.

The second section, beginning with verse 7, deals with the Christians' practice of their religious and theological life:

1. Those who had had spiritual rule over them were to be remembered, knowing that they gave their lives for Christ.

2. The readers are to watch that they remain sound in the faith and not be carried away by "every wind of doctrine." In order to live that way the readers were to lead a separate life and come out from the camp of Judaism, discarding the old legalistic way.

3. There is an altar, for the exclusive use of the saints, which may be the cross of Christ, on which He shed His blood for us. Those who do service at the tabernacle and adhere to the legal, Judaistic practices have no right to claim any part of the work of that altar. These readers are still in danger of "working out their salvation" by the works of the law, and as long as they continue to do so they will never be saved by Jesus Christ.

There is a fine distinction between "in the camp," which was the temple where the religionists — the scribes and Pharisees — held sway, and "without the camp," where Jesus Christ shed His blood and died. If anyone wanted to stay in the camp, he would not be saved; for only those who came to Jesus outside the camp obtained remission of sin through the blood He shed there. Today those for whom Christ died go outside the camp — not to earn salvation, but to accept its blessings as a free gift. Because we are saved by grace we should now offer up a sacrifice of praise to God for so great a salvation.

William R. Newell writes, "Six words might sum up the believing Hebrew's position: *'Within the veil'* (6:19; 10:20); *'without the camp.'* 'Within the veil' is the heavenly position: Christ is there, and believers in fact are there in Him, and are to be there in constant entrance (10:19 ff.). 'Without the camp' reveals where Christ is and His followers are, as to this world and its 'religion' " (*Hebrews*, p. 451).

Another "let us" passage begins with verse 13. We are to go to Him without the camp and bear His reproach. Obviously this does not mean that we are to go this time for salvation. The readers already possessed that. But because those readers seemed to be mixing Judaism with Christianity, the writer exhorts them to go away from Judaism and break with it. In doing so they would be reproached by those who remained in the camp, the unsaved religionists. But these saved ones should expect that kind of treatment because Jesus Christ had literally been cast outside the camp by them also. Those who do go outside the camp will bear His reproach, which means that the hate and spite the Jews heaped on Jesus will now be heaped on the believers.

By going outside the camp the believers prove that they no longer trust in Levitical sacrifices, but trust entirely in the sacrifice of Jesus Christ. The Christians will offer sacrifices, but only the sacrifices of thanks and praise. The proof that they are offering such sacrifices will be seen in doing good and in good fellowship. The Christians who do this will see that they are separated, in a sense from all that has been dear; but they will be compensated by a loving fellowship with Christ and with one another. The kinship of Christians in some instances is closer than the tie of earthly bonds of blood.

When one is outside the camp he certainly will be called on to make sacrifices. This time he will not offer the blood of goats and rams, but a living sacrifice. This sacrifice is really threefold: (1) our person; (2) our praise; (3) our pocketbook.

One will never give the second and third until the first is completely presented, as stated by Romans 12:1, 2. Because the person is offered, the other two will follow. One may well question the reality of the first if the second and third are not present. If the pocketbooks are closed to God and opened only to self, and lips are closed to praise and open to shame, sham, criticism, and earthly and sinful words, we had better examine whether we are in the faith.

The Conclusion

The conclusion of the entire book begins either at verse 18 — if you wish to make it a personal conclusion, saying that the writer does not want to include that in the body of the book — with a request for prayer for him and others with him; or, it begins with verse 20, which is the glorious benediction. Technically, the conclusion begins with verse 20, while verses 18 and 19 are parenthetical.

The writer concludes: "The God of peace . . . make you perfect in every good thing." In Scripture God is often called "the God of love" (II Cor. 13:11; I John 4:7). Here, however, the emphasis is on peace, the gift of God's love. Further, God (Jesus Christ) is set forth in His resurrection and is called the "great shepherd of his sheep." Jesus Christ is the great shepherd and the resurrected shepherd. The third thought in the conclusion is the eternal covenant.

The covenant concept is found frequently in the Bible. There is an eternal covenant that God made, and it was manifested in time to Abraham and carried out in time through the sacrifice of Jesus Christ. This covenant depends not at all on us, but exclusively on Jesus Christ. It is sealed and confirmed eternally and the guarantee comes from the eternal God. This covenant will be kept by the God of peace. This covenant is a covenant between the God of peace and the great shepherd of the sheep. The God of peace is so called because His intentions are love and peace, and these intentions are carried out with the shepherd who by His death saved us. It is on the basis of the blood of that eternal covenant that we are made perfect, and not through Levitical sacrifices or through anything within ourselves such as good works. So important is the covenant concept in the mind of the writer that even in his conclusion he makes reference to the covenant so that it will remain firmly in their minds.

The last few verses are still exhortation. Because there has been much exhortation in the book and because people are apt not to appreciate exhortations, the writer asks them to bear with him.

For us today the impact of the message of Hebrews can be summed up in a quotation taken from the *Missionary Monthly* of October, 1968, which in turn is quoting an EPA Syndication Article of August, 1968, written by D. Elton Trueblood. The last paragraph of this reads, "Committed Christians are a minority today in all countries, including the United States. There is no possibility that a minority can survive unless it is tough-minded and able to continue in spite of ridicule. But such tough-mindedness cannot be produced except on the basis of disciplined living. Therefore the return to Christian discipline is a tremendous basis of hope."

The work closes on a warm personal note, with greetings extended to the dedicated workers and believers as well as a note about Timothy, who had been freed from jail and was thinking of visiting the Hebrew Christians — at Jerusalem perhaps. The destination of this letter is not really known. "Those of Italy salute you" might indicate that the letter was written to Christians from Rome. The fact is, however, that most scholars think "Italians" were citizens outside of Rome, a band of them, perhaps with Apollos as their minister.

Included in the closing statement is that characteristic mark which is one of the Christian attributes: "Grace be with you all. Amen." What better way could one conclude? That word of Scripture comes, not from the writer, first of all, but from the God whom we honor, love, and serve because of Christ's great gift to us. To all of us, then, to whom Jesus Christ is the supreme, majestic, and personal Savior and mediator, in whom we indeed have better Christian living, comes this benediction from the God of peace — "Grace be with you." To live in His grace is better Christian living indeed, but it is also the best and only way of life. Better Christian living indeed when God's love given to us through the precious blood of the eternal high priest, Jesus Christ, the mediator of a better covenant, carries with it peace and joy abounding. The price in terms of sacrifice may be high, but the rewards are abiding and infinite. To live in that way is indeed life eternal. Christ, through the Holy Spirit working in us, assures of continued and certain victory.

Lesson 16
Questions, Topics, Suggestions for further study

1. Is chapter 13 mostly doctrinal or mostly practical? Prove your point of view with evidence from the chapter.

2. Memorize, write out, and give reasons why verse 8 and verses 20, 21 are considered highlights of this closing chapter.

3. With what twofold exhortation does the chapter open?

4. With what three aspects of our religious life does the second part of the chapter open?

   a.

   b.

   c.

5. Tell of the distinction between "in the camp" and "without the camp."

6. In view of Jesus' having given His life "without the camp," what is our duty?

7. What sacrifices are Christians called to make?

8. How does the conclusion (vss. 20-21) designate God?

9. Write a paragraph on "the eternal covenant."

10. What does this writer wish his readers to do about all the exhortations he has given them?